"John has been one of those used of God to bring me into these life-giving truths of grace and our identity in Jesus. He is my friend. You will feel he is yours as you read these real-life stories of redemption."

~ Bart Millard of MercyMe

"Everyone I know wants to hang out with John Lynch. He's just that type of guy. You're drawn to him, almost without explanation. Maybe it's because he's so uniquely gifted, but more likely it's because he makes you feel important. John Lynch is raw. John Lynch is real. And most importantly, John Lynch knows Jesus. This book is your chance to hang out with John, share some incredibly honest moments with him, and discover the rejuvenating power of God's grace."

~ Dr. Andrew Farley, host of Andrew Farley LIVE on Sirius XM, bestselling author of *The Naked Gospel* and *Twisted Scripture*

"John Lynch is a trusted storyteller who brilliantly engages the human journey, both his and ours, with kind humor, authentic insight, and deep compassion."

~ Paul Young, author of *The Shack*, *Cross Roads*, *Eve*, and *Lies We Believe About God*

"I urge you to listen to your heart and accept John's invitation in his book to experience, as he is, God's amazing grace."

~ Bill Thrall, co-founder of Trueface, co-author of *The Cure*

"I have never met anyone like John Lynch. He reminds me of a human lantern shining a light of God's outrageous love so bright my eyes squint. If you are so lucky as to read the magnificent *On My Worst Day*, you will encounter an unguarded peek into a life compellingly marked by unfathomable grace, and the vast love of a very intimate God. Let these powerful words shine as they persuade all of us who long for redemption in our own stories: 'Not a minute left to chance, not a moment uncared for.' Cheers to this important and hopeful book!"

~ Tracy Levinson, bestselling author of *Unashamed - Candid Conversations about Dating, Love, Nakedness, & Faith*

"John has the gift of story! Very few can connect with people's hearts the way John can using story, his story. John has truly hit this one out of the park. Reading how God takes days in the life of John Lynch and turns them into redemptive pieces of art makes me want to grab a coffee, or a beer, and sit in a quiet place to read, cry, smile, laugh, and thank God for my own story. I now see the redemptive power of Jesus at work in my own life! Thank you, John! You give hope to so many!"

~ Jeremy Affeldt, three-time World Champion pitcher for the San Francisco Giants, founder of Generation Alive

"There is nothing more beautiful than when someone lets you into their private world. *On My Worst Day* does just that! John Lynch brings life and beauty to God's amazing grace for us all.

~ Jan Dravecky, speaker and co-author of *When You Can't Come Back*, and Dave Dravecky, retired major league pitcher for the San Francisco Giants. Co-founders of Endurance.

"John's way of explaining grace—what it is, what it's not, and what it can do for me—saved my life."

~ Bob Ryan, author of *Signs Along the Road*

On My Worst Day

The Narrative Changes
When Redemption Enters In

JOHN LYNCH

Scripture taken from the Holy Bible, New American Standard version, NASB.

Book + Jacket design by Lazarus Media Productions
Printed in the USA
First Printing, 2020

ISBN 978-1-7752468-9-3 (paperback)
ISBN 978-1-7752468-8-6 (ebook)

Published by Lazarus Media Productions
www.lazarusmediaproductions.com

In This Book

Foreword

IF YOU'RE LOOKING for a writer to share all his secrets for unlocking the doors to conquering life and every struggle you've ever wrestled with, John Lynch is probably not your man.

But...

If you're looking for someone to walk beside and encourage you, while ruthlessly admitting his own temptations and weakness, John Lynch might just be the man you're looking for. I suppose I could say, John is so fully sure of God's love for us, he is able to fully display what being human is to us.

I first met John years ago at an event with a few other bands including my own. I was immediately struck by his lack of pretense, his love for story, and his easy ability to convey deep and moving empathy. Whether communicating on stage or listening to someone's problem backstage, John quickly convinced me that he poignantly understands what it means to become a safe place. Having played concerts in somewhere around a few thousand churches, I think it's safe to say I've met my fair share of "celebrity" pastor types. For better or worse, I'm no longer easily dazzled, nor do I care to be.

I once heard Jeff Goldblum say in an interview that the secret to acting isn't to be interesting or fascinating, it's to be interested and fascinated.

I think you'd agree, we are drawn to those who don't merely want us to see how great *they* are, but instead, invite us to see, with them, just how great *God* is.

In fact, the more stages I've stepped onto, the less I want to be impressed and the more I hunger for communicators who are willing to share the gospel with unyielding vulnerability.

John is one of those mesmerizing few who not only possesses the rare ability to deeply see *his* audience but is actually willing to be seen *by* his audience.

On My Worst Day is no exception.

Through a myriad of personal stories, coupled with rare gospel-saturated honesty, John is able to not only convince us that he could be loved on his worst day but so can we.

~ Mike Donehey of Tenth Avenue North

It Begins...

I WAS RUNNING with everything in me. The wind coming through the earholes in my helmet was so loud, I wondered if people in the stands could hear it. It felt like everything in my life depended upon my sliding into third base safely. Every day, something felt this important…

On that day, the good guys won. I hit a triple and scored the go-ahead run. And on that late spring afternoon, my team, the Upland Lions, defeated Boyd Lumber 6–3, at Olivedale Park.

The teams shook hands, the coach talked to us for a few minutes, then everyone packed up and headed home.

It was now two-something. I was sitting on top of a picnic bench, in my sticky wool uniform, baking in the bright sun.

My mom was late again.

Everyone had left the stadium. The maintenance man graded the field, locked up the snack booth, and had now driven off. I was officially the last witness at the scene.

The year was 1964.

I'd been staring into my glove and picking mud off my cleats. Then I started trying out different sounds and voices. I was bored. I was rarely bored. But the heat and glare were taking their toll. There was little shade yet at this recently built park.

Then suddenly, it happened. Without planning it, I found myself talking to God.

I'd never done it before that moment.

God, so I think You should know, I'm on to You. I know something's up. I know You're real. The other night, I was walking home in the dark. I saw things in the shadows that didn't look right. Someone was following me. I was scared. So scared. I didn't know if I should knock on a neighbor's door or start trying to outrun whoever it was until I got home.

In that moment I called for someone I couldn't see. I whispered, "Help!" That was You, wasn't it?

Why did I call out to You? My family doesn't believe in You. We are Unitarians, I think. I don't know what that means. But my dad says You don't exist. He says leaders made You up so people would behave better.

Anyway, I felt something I don't know how to describe. I haven't talked to anyone about it. I've never felt anything like it before. I want my whole life to be that way—the way it was during those two minutes. I want it to come back so much.

So, who are You?

I see paintings and statues at churches. That can't be You. You look terrible! They make You look angry or sad or like You need some food. You have this look, like You're expecting us to do something. And nobody seems to be able to figure out what You want. And none of it matches what I felt walking home the other night.

And church people. I don't get them at all. They seem so strange to me. They're trying too hard or something. Like they're trying to convince themselves they're better than others. Maybe they are, but I would never want to be like them. Their smiles don't seem real.

Anyway, I don't know what to do next. Don't forget me. I know what I felt that night was real. I wanted You to know I know. Thanks for making the people in the bushes go away.

Then a horn honked. It was my mom, in our 1957 Chevy Biscayne.

That was the last time I would talk to Him or think much about Him for nearly two decades.

That boy was me, John Lynch. What follows is the chronology of figuring out how to make real the life I experienced, for several minutes, that night in the dark. My story seems to follow this progression:

- The first part of my life I spent trying to make myself lovable so I would be loved.
- The second part of my life I spent trying to make myself worthy of the love I had found.
- The third part of my life I spent trying to convince myself the love I had found was enough.
- This fourth part of my life I am actually beginning to experience the life love has given me.

So, I'm writing this book—for us. To help us believe God is daily drawing us to receive a life magnificently worthy of His love.

A life which will hold up—on my worst day. Maybe you too will find yourself on these pages.

For He has heard your call in the dark, too… Even on your worst day.

December
1958

THE FIRST CHRISTMAS gift I can remember was a rubber-tipped bow and arrow set.

During the Eisenhower administration, it was maybe the finest gift available to a five-year-old. I tore into the cellophane-wrapped package and sprinted into the neighborhood to show off my six arrows and bow. I proudly carried it all in the provided plastic quiver, transported with a functional twined strap.

Our family celebrated Christmas earlier in the morning than most. So, at 7:30, I was not as welcomed into neighborhood homes as I had hoped. I was left alone to hunt imaginary weasels in my Allentown cul-de-sac.

That's when I wandered by the only manhole on our street. I had no reason to believe it wasn't the only one in the free world. One of the neighborhood kids' uncle told him if you dropped a stone into the manhole, got real quiet, and waited long enough, you could hear a person in China swear in their own language. He reasoned China was exactly across the world from us and that they didn't yet have manhole covers. Only the holes. My friends and I spent many hours around our manhole cover, to see if we could make it happen. But so far, nothing. Sitting there, now, with my bow and arrows, in front of the manhole, I began to wonder if perhaps an item with more substance would better make the journey.

This next section of this story, I still can't get my head around.

Without giving myself a chance to question my impulse, I slid one of the arrows into the tiny manhole cover hole and let it go. I listened. It made several indistinguishable sounds and then… silence. Nothing conclusive. So, I tried another. And another. Eventually, I put all my arrows down that manhole. I may have jammed the bow down there too. I had to go home without my bow and arrow set. The same boy who had left with a bow and arrow set.

Later, upon questioning, I panicked and told my parents Dougie Herring had forcibly taken my arrows and put them down our manhole. He was an easy mark. Nobody liked Dougie Herring. Even his parents didn't believe Dougie's defense. That night he got the spanking of his life.

If I hadn't known before, I knew it then. I was capable of great wrong.

I laid in bed that night wondering to myself, *What in the world happened today? Did I actually throw my entire bow and arrow set down a manhole?*

I didn't yet have anyone I could trust to talk about this with, except myself. And I didn't want to talk about it. So I stuffed it. I would learn to become a very skilled stuffer over time.

I walked out my door the next morning as a kid who had thrown his prized possession down a manhole and then blamed a friend for it.

Welcome to my world.

John, you will not yet be able to hear these words, but starting today I will speak to you for the rest of your life. We can play the highlights over again when you get home. For now, they will cause you to sense something beyond your own voice when you go to bed tonight. When you finally do hear Me, twenty-three years from now, you'll find it familiar enough to trust.

So, here we go.

You are correct. Today was an odd one for you. I understand all things and I'm still not entirely certain what that was all about! The entire set of arrows? Really?

But know this: from before the world began, I wanted there to be an exact you on this planet. I picked for you to arrive in this city, Allentown, Pennsylvania. Someday, you will travel to where you were told those arrows went.

Yes, you will do bizarre stuff like this again. On a winter's day, five years from now, you will bury a brand-new sweater, which you actually like, between second and third on a local baseball field. In your forties, I will have to stop you from throwing your keys overboard during a choppy ride in a friend's boat. You will reason, because you have no pockets in your swimsuit, your keys eventually will fly from your hands into the lake. Trying to avoid this tension, you will actually consider beating fate to the punch.

Even this bizarre quirk is all part of the way I created you. You'll add your own peculiar twists to it. But know this: I am never disgusted or embarrassed of who you are. Not now, not later, not ever.

Oh, and you're going to take us to some very odd places. So, cut yourself some slack. We're just getting started on this ride. Yes, I'm aware of the lying. And I see you stuffing feelings away and going private with what confuses and embarrasses you. But yours is a book with many chapters. I'm going to need some time...

1960

AMONG A KID'S highest motivations is to avoid embarrassment. Most parents want to keep their kids from it. But all parents sometimes miss the narrative. And when kids get embarrassed publicly, it's not pretty.

Case in point: My parents got me my first bike in 1960. It was gigantic! The seat almost came up to my shoulders. What were they thinking? Dad must have gotten it for nearly free. We weren't poor but the Depression taught him utility over style.

He taught me to ride a bike on one that was built for a grown man likely delivering artillery shells during the war, not a bike built for a child in peacetime.

As he hoisted me up onto the bike, he'd grunt, "Let's do this, young man." He'd push me for a few steps and then let go. The first couple of attempts I thought he was running alongside, helping me balance.

He wasn't.

I learned how to steer from the motivation of horror. Inside I was shrieking, *I'm going to die! I'm going to die!* The bike was so heavy, once it got moving, only a parked car could stop it. (I know this from experience.) I couldn't fully reach the pedals. I just had to aim myself towards a hedge and brace for pain. Or, like a pilot running out of gas, at the last moment I'd stretch out my leg, skidding and jerking, until a knee, freshly embedded with asphalt would grind me to a halt. I could have been crippled for life! Parents taught their kids to ride like this in the '60s—loving parents! I'm not kidding. No wonder the life expectancy was lower then.

After five or six such attempts, my dad was convinced I could ride. "Son, I think you've got the hang of it."

What?! I couldn't even touch the pedals!

But I wasn't about to tell him I couldn't yet ride and risk being shot out of a cannon again into Mr. Cutler's station wagon.

Predictably, on normal-sized bikes, my friends had all learned to ride. They'd fly by my house, in packs, with playing cards in their spokes, "Come on, Lynch! Get your bike!" Even Leslie Gabbon was riding her bike, and I'd always been told she only had one good eye!

I made excuses and probably feigned illness in an effort to avoid having to ride. Then one morning, I got an idea. *Hey, wait, I can walk my bike! If people see me walking my bike around the neighborhood, maybe they'll think I can ride, but wanted to walk the bike for a bit instead.*

So I walked my bike one street over, to the cul-de-sac where most of my friends congregated.

Soon, everyone was on bikes, circling around me, "Let's go, Lynch!" I balked.

Then someone called out, "I don't think you can ride your bike." Another started to sing, "John can't ride his bike. John can't ride his bike." (Kids can be cruel. Even if you're well-liked.)

I knew I had to interrupt before things got out of control. "Yeah, well, I can ride my bike. I just don't want to." I actually said that. Out loud.

Memory has mercifully blocked out the few days that followed.

Someone probably let me try their bike, and I *did* learn to ride. I'm certain there's a great insight I could include at this point... But all I knew was that when the time came, my kids would have bikes that fit them. And they would learn to ride in a quiet corner of a park, not on an asphalt mosh-pit, in front of kids they'd have to see for the next dozen years. It's hard enough for a kid to face life with good equipment.

Decades later, I would coach my son's Little League team. One kid would show up to practice the first day with a plastic glove. A plastic baseball glove. Perhaps a single mother, knowing nothing about baseball got him a glove at a grocery store. Before I would be able to get him a real glove, he'd stop coming to practice. He never had a chance.

. . . Awakening . . .

Self-protection becomes our default once we no longer believe adults can be trusted to protect us. It is what will draw us to Jesus. He never loses the narrative of our hearts' story.

. . . .

1960

I WAS SITTING in my parents' 1957 green Chevy Biscayne in the Upland, California, Shopping Bag Market parking lot. I was barely old enough to be left alone in the car. It's a field day for a kid to be given free rein in his parents' car! I could make so many buttons and knobs do cool things. There used to be cigarette lighters in cars. I put my finger onto the orange-hot coil. That was a mistake. I spit on my finger and kept working my way around the dash. I ran the wiper blades. I spun the dial across the radio. I honked the horn, making shoppers jump as they carried groceries past our car. I thought, *I must be the funniest boy in town!*

After a while it dawned on me, my parents had been inside the store for a long time. Uncomfortably long. *What could take so long in a grocery store? You buy your stuff and check out. It's not like there's a theater in there!* I fiddled a while longer with mirrors and seat adjustments. Still no parents. Then this: *What if they're so sick of being my parents, they've planned this opportunity to slip out the back? They're willing to give up the car and their home and spend the rest of their lives on the run if they can get away from me.* I was seven, maybe eight; and in that moment, this was the most logical, reasonable explanation I could come up with. Where does that come from?

My parents loved me. On occasion, they told me. They fed me and washed my clothes. They signed me up for school and took me to Dodger games. But my best explanation for them being too long in a grocery store was child abandonment. I was strategizing my next few hours as an orphan when they walked out. I realize now how deeply this runs in my DNA. Nothing really sad, no traumatic rejection had yet happened to me. No relatives had died. I didn't like girls yet. But this internal voice played, without sleep: *Something about you, John, is fundamentally wrong. Given enough time, people will reject you. Others aren't like you. They are normal and worth loving. Apparently, you are neither. Figure out some reason to be loved; some talent to keep people around, or this is going to be a very lonely and hard life.*

In a hundred different ways I can still create scenarios of impending abandonment. Now it's my wife, or those closest to me.

I wonder if all of us, early on, experience something similar. Some go my route. Others pretend they are superior and everyone else is suspect. Either way, we're all bluffing, whistling in the dark, until something or someone comes to convince us of our actual worth.

On My Worst Day

1962

OUR PRINCIPAL AT Baldy View Elementary walked into my fourth-grade class like she was about to announce one of our students had landed on the moon. She called Susan Sato up front. "Students, several weeks ago, Susan turned this quarter into the office. She found it on the playground and wanted to make sure it got to the person who lost it. We waited to see if anyone would come looking for it. Today, I return this quarter to you, Susan, with great appreciation for your honesty." The whole room applauded like she'd been awarded the medal of distinguished service. She was like a hero at our school for the next few weeks. Kids would ask to see the famous quarter.

That evening, I took a five-dollar bill from my mom's wallet. I didn't think she'd notice and I'd have it back to her soon enough, along with some world-class praise and attention for her son.

I turned in the bill to the office. "I found this out on the playground. I was going to take it home but I thought someone might miss it if it was theirs."

The lady at the front desk was not impressed. She appeared inconvenienced.

Wait, I thought. *Where's the principal?*

I wanted to ask for the money back and return at a more strategic time. "How long before, well, we know if someone claims it?"

She was vague, "If the principal comes to your class, you'll know."

"So, you'll be sure to keep it safe and stuff, um, in case someone wanted to claim it?" She shrugged more than nodded.

I waited… And waited… And waited. Every day for five weeks I prepared myself for the principal's arrival to my classroom. Imagine, if a quarter got such a response, what five dollars would get me!

The principal never came.

Finally, I went to the office and asked, "So, I turned in a five-dollar bill a while ago. I was just wondering when the principal will be coming to our class."

The same lady at the front desk looked at me coldly. "Oh. Someone claimed that. Thanks."

I was devastated. I wanted to yell out, "Hey, lady, that was *my* money! The only person who could claim it to be lost was *me*. And the only one who knew about it was you. You took my money, you old hag!"

But I knew she had me. If she told the principal I brought my own money in to get back and be awarded for, I'd be in big trouble.

I walked backward out of the office, glaring at her. She held eye contact with a forced smile which said, "I've already spent your money, you little chump."

Two lessons emerged from the experience. First, I realized adults in roles of authority do not always have your best interest at heart.

And I freshly discovered the lengths I would go to be adored and praised. I never told my mom. I only learned to bury deeper the truth of what I was capable of doing.

John, I know what happens from here. You will want to dig yourself deeper into shame. You stole money from your mom and then lost what belonged to her to a dishonest person. You took from your parents so you could get from your friends.

...I get it. I watched it. But this is not the whole story. I've built into you a longing to have your life count, to be affirmed for giving away what I've given you. You just don't know how to do it yet. In your immaturity, this looked like a quick way to fill that longing. You will walk down tens of dozens of blind alleys before you are convinced none of these false attempts will give you what you're looking for. Even if the principal had given you the money, it wouldn't have paid off. I've built life that way. You can get everything, climbing to the top of the heap, but I will always be the only one who can couple the experience with joy.

I will direct your parents to buy a few acres of land in a few years, which will more than compensate for what you lost. It wouldn't hurt you to voluntarily do something around the house. It might make you feel better until you understand how forgiveness and repentance work.

I do have to say, you had a very creative plan. Some kids might think to do it, but you actually tried it! It was terribly flawed. But had that front desk lady been honest you might have pulled it off. Nothing's changed between us. I saw this one coming for a long time.

So, there I was, already fully locked into this reality: **The first part of my life I spent trying to make myself lovable so I would be loved.**

1962

MR. YUKECH PASSED away from kidney failure that year. He lived across the street, on Altura Way. For some reason, he took a kind interest in me. If he saw me playing out front, he'd usually walk over. We'd sit for hours on our front stoop. Who does that? A sixty-some-year-old and a kid spending unhurried chunks of time together. With him, I felt known, even not talking at all. I think, all along, he was trying to convince me I was worth his time. Like that single gift would help me.

He had no idea how much it would.

He talked to me about life, about nearly everything. He was wise. I listened to him, because even then I could tell he wasn't giving adult slogans. He listened to me, like what I was saying was important. He was real. Most adults saw me as a disrespectful, spoiled punk. So did Mr. Yukech. But he was able to see over it all. He gave me my first baseball glove. He restrung one from his garage and rubbed saddle soap into every crevice. I'd give up a lot to have that glove today. During my entire childhood, he was the only adult I visited in a hospital. I made my parents drive me there. When he ultimately passed away from kidney failure, it was the first time I'd experienced deep loss.

When I eventually did start to risk trusting others, it was largely because I'd once known someone trustworthy. I would waste far too much of my life in foolishness, without wisdom, fighting this truth:

... *Awakening* ...

Anyone can get knowledge and information; but nobody gets wisdom, insight, and discernment without trusting.

. . . .

Ever since Mr. Yukech, I was looking hard for such a place.

John, I will make sure Bill Yukech sees this piece.

1962

I HAVE NEVER known anyone with a more beautiful heart than my mom. She was a language teacher and a linguist. At the time of her death, she was writing a book on root similarities of the romance languages. She sang opera professionally. She was the kindest, most other-centered person I have ever met.

I was always told both my parents were atheists. But I have this memory. It still makes me cry. One evening my dad and I got into an argument over something. I was sent to my room—livid, shaking, fighting back tears until I got out of his presence. Later, my mom knocked on the door of my room, entered, and sat next to me on my bed. She stroked my hair and eventually whispered "John, there's a place coming where there are no tears and the real you will be fully known. There is one who will make sense of all the pain. I promise you."

It was unlike anything she'd ever said to me. We never spoke of it again. I never knew what to do with it. I've wondered if those words guided me to Him. I picture her in heaven.

John, sometimes people trust Me early on and then their lives gets misdirected. They marry someone who doesn't trust Me. Or the melody gets lost amid pain. But I don't forget. No matter how faint, distorted or convoluted, I can ferret out trust. I gave you an astoundingly good mother. You did not yet know how to return her love. You were a kid. But she knows now. I want you to know that. I've not forgotten and she knows. That's as far as we can go right now. Her words set you on a journey for the land and person she described. You will be twenty-five when she leaves this world. You will lay sprawled out on a boulder in the middle of a Connecticut forest, crying out to whoever holds forever. You will beg and demand and shout to be assured she is safe. You will ache for there to be a God—a good and real and powerful God. You will tell Me what she said that evening on your bed... John, I missed not one word. I was there, on the boulder with you. And I do only right.

Fall, 1962

LET ME PAUSE and insert a thought from near the end of this book. In my sixties, I would go to a counselor for the first time in my life. At some point, he would walk me through an exercise.

"John, try to imagine yourself, sometime in the past, in the safest place you can think of." I'd select the fall of 1962. I envisioned myself out in the front yard, at night, laying in the grass, after playing football by myself. I was wearing a Pendleton flannel shirt, tossing a football up in the air and catching it.

"Now, John, try to place Jesus somewhere nearby." After a few moments, I'd respond, "I'm imagining Jesus lying comfortably next to me, His arms behind His head, looking up into stars He created."

The counselor asked, "What would that nine-year-old boy want to ask Him?"

I started crying before I could get words out. "Am I going to be okay? Jesus, am I going to be okay?" I sobbed for five minutes before I spoke again. Stacey was sitting next to me, stroking my hand.

I guess this entire book is an answer to that question, "Am I going to be okay?" I wish I had someone I could have asked that question of throughout my childhood, into high school, and beyond. It takes a lot of courage to intentionally examine the timeline of our lives here on earth and look for His presence, protection, and perfect love. But He promises that He won't, and will not, ever leave us nor forsake us. It is a sacred gift to know that, maybe, even before we knew Him, He heard our voices from early on, and has spent every moment since answering them with a perfect love unique to each of us. Maybe my journey will give you a chance to go back and rehearse it all; this time with Jesus, lying on your backs, looking up together into the sky He created.

October 2
1963

I LOVED SCHOOL. I really did. But I loved the Dodgers more than I can express. And Sandy Koufax was my hero. The Dodgers and Koufax were in the 1963 World Series. This was some of the earliest proof to me that there might be a God.

It was October 1st. The next day, Sandy Koufax was set to pitch against Whitey Ford in Game One! They would play in Yankee Stadium at 1 p.m. Unfortunately, that was 10 a.m. in Upland, California where I lived.

Back in the '60s, teachers played the World Series games on television sets, in their classrooms. Every classroom. Every game. At least that's how it was at Baldy View Elementary. When and why did they stop doing that?

Anyway, as much as I appreciated the gesture, most of the kids in my class didn't follow the Dodgers like I did. There would be too much talking going on—I needed to watch this one by myself. But how? My parents never let me skip school for any reason. Except if I was really sick. They were both academics. Education was amongst their highest values.

So, I devised a plan…

The morning of October 2nd finally arrived… It was 6:45 a.m. Dad had already left for work. Mom had been by my room. Twice. "Time to get up for school, John," she called as she walked by my door.

I waited. It was now 6:55 a.m. I was strategically still in my pajamas. Mom was now in the kitchen making breakfast. It was time to make my move.

What happened next is the stuff that makes great criminal legends shake their heads in reverential awe.

It wasn't convincing enough to tell my mom that I was sick. I needed her to figure out my sickness on her own. I snuck into the hall bathroom and began filling the bathtub with water. I knew people usually threw up in the toilet, but I couldn't figure out how to make that work—flushing a toilet would give her nothing to work with. So, I pretended I'd just thrown up while kneeling over the bathtub.

I called out, "Mom! Mom?" My plea was delivered in a weak, sickly sounding voice. She walked in to see me on my knees, leaning over the tub, quietly clearing my throat. As planned, she interpreted that the running water was washing down the last of my throw up. She immediately put her hand on my back and said kindly, "Oh, my. You just threw up. I'm so, so sorry. Well, young man, you are not going to school today. Do you understand?"

"Yes. I guess so," I replied.

Mom gently helped me up, saying, "Alright. Let's get you back into bed, mister. I'll get a bowl to put beside your bed. And let's get some fluids into you." I slowly acted my way back to my bed. I even mixed in a bit of a limp. (Perhaps a bit much.) She returned in what seemed like moments, placing a TV tray next to my bed. She poured me a glass of ginger ale. Why did my parents always have ginger ale in the fridge? None of us drank it unless we were sick. And the Lynchs were rarely sick.

The wheels were in motion.

8:30 a.m. came.

Mom entered my room. "I've prepared the couch for you if you want to come out and watch some television. It might cheer you up."

"Maybe a little later. I'm going to try and sleep," I answered in a sleepy voice.

"That's a good idea, young man. Get some sleep and come out to the living room when you wake up."

I entered the living room in time for the first pitch. Koufax struck out the first five batters he faced. Fifteen overall! The Dodgers beat the Yankees that day 5-2, with Johnny Roseboro hitting a home run.

At the end of the game, Mom walked in. "Well, young man, you're looking much better."

Then this next moment happened. She looked at the TV and then slowly back to me. After a few moments of pause, she said, "Your dad called a bit ago. I told him you were sick. He mentioned the Dodgers are in the World Series. Is that the game you were just watching? Come to think about it, you've been talking about this series quite a bit. What a coincidence to get sick on this day."

Well, I'll be!

My mom was on to me. In that moment, we both knew that the other knew. I think she may have been on to me from the time she walked into the bathroom. How cool was she? She endured my bad acting all day, allowing me to think I was playing her. Where did she learn that from? Love taught it to her. My parents didn't raise me to lie. But in the case of Koufax and the Dodgers in the World Series, she and I learned the dance.

I love you, Mom.

On My Worst Day

February 9
1964

ON THIS EVENING, The Beatles, in their first visit to America, appeared on *The Ed Sullivan Show*; 728 people witnessed the event in Studio 50. Seventy-four million of us stared at it on television. Most of us would never be the same. I sat there, transfixed, as though watching a talent show from another galaxy. The next morning, at school, no one greeted each other without the next sentence containing the words "The Beatles."

For me, it was so much more than the excitement of a once-a-century phenomenon. It was my indelible introduction to a lifelong obsession with becoming famous.

I soon bought a Beatles wig and was singing "It Won't Be Long" into the stereo speakers in our den—imagining I was lead singer and rhythm guitarist in a band which would eventually eclipse the popularity of The Beatles.

For my audience, I usually pictured my teachers and all those who did not understand or appreciate me. Now they were leaning over to each other between songs, confessing, "I was wrong. This young man is so incredible. I always knew it, really." So, there you go. It's not The Beatles' fault. It was in me before they showed up. For a long time, I would feel the need to prove a worth that matched my need to be loved.

It's a chump's bet, a longing that can never pay off. Even if people get it, they then wish they didn't have it. As Steve Martin writes, "At first I was not enough famous, then I was too famous, now I'm just right famous."[1]

Even today, I can't defend my motives at any given time. I used to rough myself up for not having more "godly" ambitions. I was fairly certain He couldn't use me if my motives weren't almost completely right.

Now though, I imagine Him saying something like this:

John, your motives will always be less than pure. I'm actually good with that. Maturity takes a lifetime. If I had to wait for humans to get their motives 80 percent right before I could work with them, soup wouldn't have yet been invented! You know what will one day change? You. Your entire wiring. Yes, you will still sometimes want to be adored by all mankind. But you will find yourself increasingly more concerned about others, about destiny, about having this life count. Don't be hard on yourself. You're right on time...

1964

AS A BOY, I remember thinking there was nothing as stupid or irrelevant as anything having to do with God. The Lynchs were atheists. Dad progressively pushed to get us away from celebrating Christmas. His ultimate dissident act was to have us open gifts the evening before. (Way to stick it to the man, Dad!) He brought home an aluminum tree in 1957 and we put it up every year through the late '70s, after over a third of the limbs no longer had tinsel. Most of our few ornaments eventually slid to the center. Other kids had sprawling, flocked trees with color wheels, popcorn, cranberries, and shiny ornaments, all animated by the warmth of nearly endless strands of lights. The Lynchs had sticks shoved into a pole, covered with shredded aluminum foil. I tried to not have friends over during December. Dad made sure we received mostly educational gifts or underwear, so we wouldn't get enthralled with the holiday. Nothing says Christmas like unwrapping a bag of thin dress socks.

As a kid, every picture or statue I saw of Jesus depressed or spooked me. His eyes followed me, like He was trying to get my attention so He could tell me off. "Hey, you, kid. Yeah, you. Look over here at Me! Wipe that grin off your face. I'm carrying the weight of the world, and you couldn't care less… I didn't come to earth for you."

I was never supposed to get Jesus. I was sure God was, as Karl Marx had said, "the opium of the people."[2] Everything about me cried out against everything to do with God.

Except this thought I couldn't turn off...

. . . Awakening . . .

No matter how diligently parents try to train a child in the absurdity of faith in God, they can't stop His voice: "What if I'm here, after all? What if I think about you every moment of the day? What if I hold that magic your heart keeps waiting to be true?"

. . . .

It followed me at night, on walks home. It stayed with me through the years when I mocked His name. I lived my entire childhood claiming to not believe in a God I secretly wanted.

1964

YOU COULDN'T WALK any significant distance in my childhood town of Upland without going through an orange grove. In the winter, the owners kept the fruit from freezing at night through a series of oil-generated, heat-producing "smudge pots." The ignited oil in those squatty metal drums placed along the rows of trees gave off a dirty, smoky warmth. The orchard formed a warm canopy and temporary home for drifters or those hiding from local authorities. What a different time it was in the world! My friends and I were always fascinated, getting to hang out with real hobos. We'd stand around them, speechless, like we were watching men from another planet.

I especially remember one in particular. He had thick oily hair, wore a flannel shirt and greasy jeans. He looked pretty beaten down. But he seemed so cool, living alone out under the sky. He was sketchy looking—pretty quiet and wearing a nervous tic. But he was kind, careful to not frighten us with the gruff realities of his journey. He showed us how to cook things with aluminum foil on an open fire. He'd grill up corn, pancakes, and pieces of what he called "sparrow meat." He sometimes whittled while he talked to us. We never once thought about any danger.

Today, imagine a kid telling his mom, "Hey, I'm going with my friends to visit a vagrant out in the orange groves. He has a knife."

It all set a course for me. It caused me to not fear those on the edges of society. Years later, I discovered the ones who talk to me most genuinely, tenderly, and authentically about God are often those having the toughest time managing daily life in society. Somehow, they manage to most clearly see God in the midst of it. This childhood freedom would teach me to give dignity with my time, attention, and presence to those who doubt their lives matter. To those whose failure and weaknesses try to convince them they are a different class of human. Great beauty doesn't avoid the most poor, fragile, or devastated. Sometimes dignity is giving importance to those who sit on the fringe. It is convincing them God loves them as well as anyone else. I think it's why I love *Cannery Row* so much. Steinbeck gave dignity to those who have no visible footing in this world. I have discovered most of my favorite speaking events have been to the painfully common, limping, and inappropriate. More often than not, they enjoy my humor the most, listen most intently to my words, and lavish me with the most pie. Maybe it's all because, behind my loud and articulate bluster, I am one of them.

I imagine that evening Jesus took Levi, the hated tax-gatherer, up on his invitation to dinner. A roomful of actively immoral outcasts, carrying all manner of visible scars of depravity, desperately trying to be on their best behavior. Quiet and awkward. If we could have filmed it, the camera would have panned in from above, through the room to where Jesus was reclining. There'd be a circle around Jesus, all of them gradually sitting up, elbows on knees, chins on hands. Hardened sinners with expressions of wonder and innocence. We'd be watching what happens when perfect love, grace, and purity invade darkness. The King had shown up to rescue prisoners from the enemy camp—where wickedness and perversion seemed logical up until that moment. Suddenly there was, at least in that room, a hope life could be different.

The night air would gradually blend into a mixture of the best humor, stories, truth, life, hope. Somewhere in the evening, the conversation would turn.

"Who are You—really?" He unhurriedly let them ask questions. Then there was silence. It was becoming clear exactly who He is. Few in the crowds outside, who sought Him for a miracle show, received what these reprobates were receiving. They were becoming desperate for who He is, not what magic He might wave.

Someone sitting next to Him asked, "Why us? Why would you choose to be here tonight, with us?"

Jesus: "This may be hard for you to understand. I've known you and loved you since before there was time. I've watched it all. I know about the catch in your knee that takes until after noon to loosen up. I was there the evenings your father beat you. I was there when you were kicked out of the synagogue. And now, I've come from heaven for you."

"But… Don't you know what I've done?"

"Yes, I do. And I have the unfortunate ability to know the wrong things you're going to do tomorrow and the day after that. The only sin which could possibly separate you from eternity with God is to reject the person who's speaking to you at this moment." He smiled. "And, I gotta tell you, I'm being welcomed here tonight like few other places since I've been down here… Now, may I finish this joke?"

And two dozen men and women, who had walked into this party ready for a fight, laughed deeply and peered into His eyes, like convicts about to receive their walking papers.

1964

FEW FOODS CAPTIVATED me in youth like cheesecake. I was always left frustrated, wanting more than I was allowed in any given sitting. My parents never allowed it into our home, treating cheesecake as a luxury only royalty should possess—like caviar or gold-leafed chocolate dishes. On the rare occasion Dad did take us to a restaurant that might carry cheesecake, he'd always make sure he pointed out the ridiculously high price of desserts. Reading the menu, he'd grumble under his breath, "These desserts cost about what I make in a day's work. What sort of people would order such a thing?"

But on my 10th birthday in 1963, he took us to the Magic Lamp— the nicest restaurant in Upland. It had white linen tablecloths and breadsticks in a basket covered with a matching linen napkin. My dad allowed me to order dessert!

When it finally arrived, it was so incredibly thin and tiny. A sliver of cheesecake, nearly lost on the dessert plate. The waiter could have served it with tweezers. I thought to myself, *I could down about nineteen of these!*

When I asked if I could have a second piece, my dad looked at me like he might give his speech about people starving in the Congo.

All of this is to help explain to you why this summer day in 1964 turned out the way it did.

I was pedaling my blue Stingray bike into downtown Upland to watch a matinee at the Grove Theater. I didn't make it that far. Turning off Euclid onto Ninth Street, I was physically pulled by what smelled like freshly baked cheesecake. The aroma came from the Upland Bakery. I was suddenly positioned in front of the glass store window in time to watch an oversized man in a white baker's uniform slide a majestic, freshly baked cheesecake from an oven with an immense wooden paddle.

(I am oft and accurately accused of runaway hyperbole, but none of what I am about to write bears the marks of such device.)

I walked into the store and up to the glass counter, on whose racks the cake had only just been placed. Pointing to it, while making eye contact with the woman behind the counter, I asked, "How much for this? How much does it cost?"

"Per slice?"

"No. The whole cheesecake. How much?"

She quoted a nearly impossible amount. But I would find a way to purchase it. The thought that I could, for once, have all the cheesecake I wanted had suddenly become the single most important goal for that day of my life.

I spoke out, clearly and slowly, "Would you please not let anyone else buy this? I'm going home to find the money to buy it. Promise?"

And I was off on my bicycle.

Mom was not home. I had eighty-five cents already on me for the movie and snacks. I dug through my dad's change cup on his dresser. I scoured every room of the house. I probably rounded up a dollar's worth of coins—still pitifully short of the amount to own that cake.

Then I remembered my Indian Head nickel collection.

A child of the Depression, my dad now had many collections—perhaps as a hedge against impending poverty. He wanted me to have a similar passion. So he had purchased a fleet of these heavy cardboard blue booklets with slots for Indian Head nickels. A slot for every year they were minted. Dad helped me get started with some fairly rare coins. I soon got into it, and in the last several years had filled many of the slots.

Somehow able to ignore perspective, consequence, and future regret, I bent back the cardboard booklets and popped out coins until I had over five dollars worth of nickels in the pockets of my jeans. I got back on my Stingray and raced to the bakery. There, I proceeded to pour out piles of nickels onto that counter.

I walked out with the entire cheesecake in a box!

I should have taken the cake home and shared half with my family. I did not do that.

I should have located a plastic fork and knife and eaten it at a local park. I did not do that.

I should have at least sat down. I did not do that.

I walked into the alley behind their store. Like a child raised by wolverines, I began breaking off huge chunks of warm, fresh cheesecake and shoving them into my mouth. It tasted so incredibly good.

For almost minutes.

To my credit, I was over halfway through the giant cake before it became oppressive. I was now slowly and reluctantly wadding it into my mouth. I started feeling sick two-thirds of the way through and tossed the rest in a dumpster several feet away.

I wandered around to the front, a boy dazed by sugar and disappointment. *What just happened?* I thought as I stared at the road, slowly weaving my bike through the neighborhoods toward home. *What will I tell Dad about the nickels? Someday he's going to want to see how the collection is coming along. Why did I do that? What is wrong with me?*

But, later that evening, an even deeper question worked its way to the surface: *Why didn't that work today? Why didn't that cheesecake make me happier?*

I don't think either of my parents ever heard this story. I can't remember how I explained the missing nickels. But I walked forward from that day, on a more urgent mission—to find what food, entertainment, activity, or repetition of activity would satisfy me long enough to quench this unmet urge inside me.

John, I do not want to rub this in; but if you'd held onto those Indian Head nickels, you could buy everyone in Upland a cheesecake… once a month… for the rest of their lives.

Trying to solve this internal craving will be the singular driving force for decades of your life. It will harm you more than any person can. It will break your heart. One day, no time soon, you will find what your longing and unmet urges are calling for. Then, you will begin to learn what gives food its maximum taste, experiences their full measure of joy, and sunsets their full beauty. I'm right here. Though you will go into some very strange places, this obsession will not destroy you. One day, your willingness to articulate your battle with it will make you safe and real and trusted to others. Until that time, you will crave the Jack in the Box taco combo like few things on earth. I'd say you could do worse, but I'm not sure I'd be accurate...

1964

THESE DAYS I cared mostly about running fast, listening to Vin Scully describe the Dodgers on the radio, and convincing enchanting Lucille Engle to like me. Orange trees still outnumbered homes. Life was pretty idyllic.

Except my fifth-grade class was run by this tough kid.

He had two older brothers who, for all I knew, were already in prison. Or should be. I didn't yet know much about evil, but his family was evil. Carl had beaten up three kids in our class and it was only October. He didn't hit me because he was entertained by me.

One day he informed me we were to meet at the railroad tracks on the coming Saturday morning. These particular tracks ran through the center of town, ending at an orange-packing plant. For us kids, that plant was a glorious place. Upland was one of the great citrus hubs. Dozens of open-topped freight cars were three-quarters filled with oranges, waiting to be sent out to places like Billings or Topeka. On late afternoons, after cul-de-sac Wiffle ball or front-yard football, dozens of us could be found lying on our backs inside train cars filled with huge, nearly fluorescent oranges. The workers didn't even care we were in there. There were so many oranges. We'd eat them until our mouths burned. Nobody had scurvy in our neighborhood.

On that Saturday, like six-dozen times before, I climbed the train's steel ladder and dove into orange heaven. But it was early Saturday morning. No one else was yet in the cars. Carl followed me in. He leaned slowly against the back wall, saying nothing. He was staring at me, intensely. I experienced the sensation of being trapped for the first time in my life.

He slowly informed me what he would now do to me, and what I would now do to him—twisted perversion I'd never before heard or thought of.

…That morning changed my life. I remember little of what happened after emerging from that boxcar: how I got home, or what I did when I got there. I have no memories of Carl after that morning. I carried this embedded maxim, which clung to me like a wet sweater all my life: *No one must ever know what happened. I will go this alone. I must find a way to never think about this again. I will be all right. I will be all right…* And a previously innocent and playful kid walked with a limp from that thought on.

I was still funny. I still seemed like a normal kid. I would pitch on my town's Little League All-Star team. Lucille Engle would like me. But something insidious was going on inside. All alone. Inside.

I've discovered since, there is a word for this silent limp: Shame.

. . . *Awakening* . . .

*Guilt says I've done something wrong. Shame
hisses there's something uniquely, irrevocably,
and fundamentally wrong with me.*

, , , , , , , , , ,

Shame tries to convince us that we caused the evil which happened to us. It continually whispers if anyone could know the truth about who we are, they would leave or pity us. So we are left to bluff and posture, guard and defend. Shame teaches us to perform for God's acceptance, to keep paying for something we eventually can no longer even name.

It would take forty years before I risked even a hint to anyone that something happened back there.

The boxcars still stand. Rusting and silent. A visible and definable part of Upland's past. My past. I've driven past them dozens of times, bringing my family to see the town of my childhood. No one in our car ever noticed me staring at those boxcars as we drove by.

Decades after that day in the boxcar, I cling to this: *Jesus, You make no mistakes; You make even better beauty out of the most heinous. You never left my side. You hated it more than I did. You give me dignity. You continue to stand with me in the arena to protect my heart and reputation. You are redeeming and will redeem all this damage. You died to take away the power of this shame. Jesus, You dropped everything to stand over me the day it all turned dark...*

1964

CHRISTMAS IS THE best holiday for kids. Hands down. But Halloween is the coolest.

In my childhood, all the kids wore their costumes to school. All day! And there was no political correctness to navigate. Nearly every ethnicity and station in society was represented and welcomed. Indian chiefs, ghosts, angels, and Vikings played kickball next to minstrels, Moses, belly dancers, sombrero-wearing Spaniards, and hobos.

In 1964, I went as the devil.

Imagine my mom at Coronet's department store, sorting through all the costumes: cowboys, doctors, astronauts. "Hmmm. Look at this. The devil. Yes, I think that's the most fitting outfit for my son. I'll get him the devil costume."

…I was so proud of her.

Trick or Treat in the '60s was so different than today's sanitized "Tribute to Harvest" or whatever it has become. Our own neighbors created haunted houses, with all manner of horrifying dramatics, designed solely to horrify children. A snarling, snapping German Shepherd might meet us at the door—within feet of us. On a leash, but still showing his teeth. Strangers would leap out of bushes with real axes or shovels in their hands, shouting at us. Then they'd laugh and hide back in the bushes for the next wave of kids. Unexplained explosions and shrieking filled the night air. No wonder my generation ends up in more counseling than any preceding it.

Old Mr. Dobbs, three houses up our street, was a Halloween legend. An odd, grumpy recluse who, on Halloween night, came to life. He positioned dry ice and cobwebs all over his compound. You could hear his eerie music and sound effects blocks away. His entire family would dress in black—each with the singular goal of scaring the pee out of children. One might jump from the roof, squirt fake blood on us from a missing arm, and then run off. Or from under a car, one would suddenly grab my foot as I walked up the driveway.

Each year Dobbs made "eyeball soup." We were certain that neighborhood cats were unwillingly involved in his recipe... I still am.

Parents didn't walk with us after, say, age six. Packs of us would roam the neighborhoods, pillowcases in hand, wearing outfits with plastic masks which caused us to keep breathing our own air.

Total strangers gave us candy! Big time candy. We might be handed two full-sized Snicker bars, without a blink.

But the best part of the whole evening was afterward. I'd haul my candy into my room, close the door, and begin the sacred candy sorting ritual. I didn't know anyone who didn't do it. There were the "A" candies: Snickers, Butterfingers, Baby Ruth bars, etc. "B" candies included Big Hunk, Mike and Ike, and the rest of that ilk. Gum, lollipops, Boston Baked Beans, and such made up the "C" category. And then there were the wretched "D" candies: candy corn and those styrofoam-like circus peanuts, with colors not found in nature.

I'd lay them all out in rows of merit and then stand back to admire my evening's effort.

The next day, upon arriving home from school, most of rows "A" and "B" and some of row "C" were gone.

Gone. Not there. Vanished.

On My Worst Day

I first blamed my brother. I even blamed my parents. It was a mystery that dragged on for months.

Until my dad's mother passed away.

She had lived her last several years with us. She and I were not especially close. Living in our den, she mostly only came out at mealtime. She was in her late eighties, which at that time was like being in her late one hundred and twenties.

One afternoon, as my parents were packing up her belongings, my mom called me into the den, "John, come look at this." And there, in the top drawer of her desk, were the wrappers and remaining pieces of uneaten candy. My candy. My grandmother had shuffled into my bedroom when no one was around and filled her spindly, saggy little arms with my candy. She probably had to make several trips. I'm not certain I've forgiven her yet.

Somehow, I wound up with her Bible. She had underlined verses and wrote the date next to them. Some of the citations were from back as far as the 1880s. I'd think to myself, "Wow, there wasn't even electric lighting yet. She'd have had to read her Bible with a kerosene lamp!" Until one day, someone mentioned in passing, "Or, maybe she read it during the day."

"Ah, yes. Perhaps she read it during the day. Certainly a viable option …"

John, I recently asked your grandmother if she ever regretted taking your candy. These are her exact words: "No. Not once. He was an annoying child. And I do so love the chocolates. No, I have no regrets."

1965

I WON THE fifty-yard dash two years in a row at Camp Oaks, up near Big Bear Lake. I still have the ribbons somewhere in my attic. No one had ever won two years in a row. And probably no one had ever made themselves more sickly nervous before a race. The rest of the kids ran because it was fun, or because they thought they had a chance to win. I ran it knowing anything but a win would be tragic. It was what I did, what I was known for. Winning that ribbon would prove for another day that I was enough. Winning it would cause me to be valued and popular. There was no other option. At that age, I thought I might be the fastest boy in my age group, anywhere. My "anywhere" was the size of Camp Oaks and the two-hundred-some campers on-site during my week.

Looking back, none of my friends were there. Most of the camp kids I never saw again. My parents thought it would be a good idea to send me to a camp. When I got home, I proudly displayed my ribbon on the living room table. My parents both nodded and smiled politely. But it wasn't that "Oh, my gosh, you're amazing!" kind of response. Dad said something like, "See, son? That's why we send you to camp. Everyone gets to win at something."

So who was I running for? I didn't enjoy a thing about the race itself. I hated the nervousness I felt for hours before it. The pushing and shoving directly before the gun sounded was chaotic and ugly. Intimidating bigger kids shuffled the weaker and smaller behind them. The race itself was only terror—two hundred screaming kids, all clawing out of the gate to take away my destiny. The honor after the race was almost nonexistent. Moments after ours, another race started, followed by another. By dinner, most of the day had blurred into one long camper decathlon.

Few seemed to even remember I'd won.

It shouldn't work like that. Greatness should be rewarded. Greatness should result in happiness. I'm sure many of the "average" kids thought I was living the dream. Turns out we were all kidding ourselves. We were all fighting our own story of insecurity. And insecurity is not solved by achievement. Insecurity is not solved by not worrying about achievement. Insecurity, it turns out, is solved only by believing the truth about how you're seen by the only one whose opinion ultimately matters… And He and I were not yet talking.

That evening, lying in my bunk, arms folded behind my head, I had felt very alone in the world.

I wish you could hear Me tonight. I will watch you repeat this cycle too many hundreds of times. I wish you could have seen what I saw today. You were magnificent! You blew everyone away and kept pulling further ahead. But you keep missing it. You were already worried about the next race before you had received the ribbon for this one. So soon, you'll be older and your knees will hurt. You'll be too heavy to want to sprint from place to place. I made you with this gift to enjoy, now. And you're missing it.

One day you will let Me in. You will discover I do not ascribe to the false story of your unacceptability. Your proving and grinding will be gradually replaced with contentment, as you begin to let Me achieve great good in you for others' benefit. That day is coming. In the meantime, though no one noticed or cared enough today, I did. I'll show you the recording when you get home. I've already shown it around here a number of times. Now go to sleep, My friend. That's another thing you won't be able to do as well when you get older.

On My Worst Day

1966

AMONG MY SIX favorite days on this planet is the one Dave Barrows and I spent in the summer of 1966. We decided to hitchhike from our home to Dodger Stadium in L.A. We never thought twice of any danger. I mean, we were nearly fourteen! I have no memory of how we got there, but vivid, Technicolor memory of nearly every moment once inside the stadium. The Dodgers were playing the Giants in a doubleheader. One price, two games. Three times the magic!

What we could afford was up in the top row of the stadium. When we finally made our way to our seats, neither of us spoke for a while. We were out of breath and deeply disappointed. Far below, the players looked like ants in uniforms.

Several minutes into trying to convince ourselves these seats would work, we decided to take a huge gamble. We had no game plan. But we would find a way down into the bottom section. The stadium was packed but we had to try. Even if we could only watch close up for an inning or two, it would be worth spending the rest of the day in a basement office with security guards.

We eventually conned our way down to the entrance of the bottom level. We didn't see anyone asking for tickets so we started our way down toward seats our own parents could never afford.

I thought we might have made it. Except this kindly looking older man, wearing a Dodger-blue straw hat, called out, "Gentlemen, excuse me. One moment."

We made the mistake of looking back.

He gestured us toward where he was standing. "May I see your tickets, please?"

"Well, um. You see, our parents are down there and…"

Dave took over, "They've got our tickets. We told them we'd be right back."

"Gentlemen, may I see your tickets?"

We each pulled out our tickets, knowing our dream was over.

He looked at them. Then he looked at us. Then he leaned his head way back, up to where our seats were. Then he looked back at the tickets. Then he looked at us again. He made a sucking sound older people make with their teeth and lips when they're considering something. He mumbled to himself. Then, very seriously he spoke, "Follow me." We did. He walked us down into the great bowl, past the wealthy people, past the players' wives, past the scouts, past the owners, all the way down to directly behind the third-base dugout. The Dodgers' dugout! Without smiling, he looked at our tickets and then at us, saying clearly and loudly, "Gentlemen, I believe these are your seats."

By the time we sat down, stared, and realized what had happened, we turned and he was gone.

We watched a doubleheader from where God sits when He watches the Dodgers play.

Koufax pitched one of the games. Sandy freaking Koufax! Maury Wills stole a base. Willie Davis dove to make a one-handed catch in center. We bought Dodger dogs and frozen malts. It was a bright, sunny Southern California summer day. We took off our shirts and swung them over our heads. We cheered like drunken sailors on leave. We listened to our hero, Vin Scully, echoing from transistor radios throughout the stadium. We'd call out the names of the players and they'd wave back. Wes Parker tipped his hat to us. We chased down foul balls. They truly were six of the finest hours of my entire life. Afterward, we waited and got autographs from Willie Davis, Bill Singer, and Al Ferrara!

For thirteen-plus years, life had been methodically teaching me the actual event never meets the anticipated expectation. But this day exceeded all anticipation. The only thing that kept it from being more perfect was the setting sun, sending us onto the freeway on-ramp and back into our normal lives.

John, I don't know who is happier this day—you or Me. I've seen this one coming for a long time. I lined up Koufax to pitch for you. That was no small feat. He was scheduled to face Marichal on Sunday. I had to give Claude Osteen a stiff shoulder so Walt Alston would be forced to move Koufax up a day.

I know you've already discovered much of life isn't as spectacular or satisfying as the anticipation. I've watched this break your heart. It will actually serve to draw you to Me. I've built into you this longing for a world which doesn't disappoint. Today, I only wanted to see you enjoying this life as completely as your being can hold. I love you a lot, kid. I can't wait until we get to meet. In the meantime, most of the day-to-day will be fine. You're going to throw a couple of no-hitters in high school. Your girlfriend will be prettier than Petula Clark. I've got a trip planned where you and a friend drive up the coast to San Francisco in your dad's Chevy Nova during college spring break. On that trip, I'll have your car break down near Santa Barbara, because I want you to get acquainted with it. You'll live on the beach there in Isla Vista during your wandering years. If you're going to run from Me, you might as well live in a nice area.

1966

IF I TELL you only what he did wrong, you wouldn't know he was a great dad. For over ten years, he quietly woke only me early each Saturday morning. Other fathers would take their sons fishing. My father took me into the kitchen, where the two of us would sit at a linoleum-laminated table, eating a thick concoction of Maypo cereal, whole milk, and serving-spoon scoops of crunchy peanut butter. You could spackle a hole in a wall with the consistency of what we ate.

On summer weekend afternoons, Dad would furtively pull two cans of Vernors out of the refrigerator—like he was handing me a dusty bottle of bootleg rum. It was only ginger ale, but he made it seem so dangerous and forbidden. Each time he'd hand it to me with these words: "Don't tell your mother."

One afternoon after work, he called me into the living room. He'd put his forefinger through a Dixie cup, and surrounded it with cotton and ketchup. He allowed me to look for a moment directly into the cup, to see a bleeding, wiggling finger. "A shop worker down at the plant cut off his finger today in one of the sheet metal machines. He told me I could bring it home and let you see it."

He was the most honest man I've known. He sacrificed incredibly for our family. He made sure we visited every state and most of the national parks in the continental U.S. He taught me to compute batting averages with a slide rule.

Before one of our vacation trips, he hid a *MAD* magazine in the glove box. He knew, at some point driving across the country, he would have to discipline me for something, and he figured we would then both retreat into hurt silence for miles. It, of course, happened. During one hideously long stretch of Midwestern driving monotony, my brother and I began bothering each other in the back seat. He flicked my ear. Twice. So, I tore a page out of what he was reading. He told on me. Dad immediately pulled off the highway. With cars whooshing by us, he completely turned around in his seat and started yelling at me. His face was bright red. He sounded like a TV preacher, bemoaning why they would spend so much money to take vacations so their kids could fight. Next thing I knew, I was in the front seat beside him. It was all painfully silent and seething, for what seemed like an hour.

Then, the moment my dad had been waiting for. Driving across the plains of Nebraska, he broke the standoff.

"You might want to check the glove box. Maybe there's something in there that might interest you."

I found the magazine... Suddenly, the last fifty miles of angry silence was forgotten. I read him sections all the way into the night, my brother and mom asleep in the backseat, on our way to that evening's Travelodge.

My father was a child of the Great Depression, the son of an uneducated immigrant who pushed a fruit cart through their eastern Pennsylvania neighborhood.

Dad was stunningly intelligent. He became a member of Mensa, "The International High IQ Society." He was in the top half of Mensa! He vowed to himself that by dogged diligence and intense focus, he would make himself someone much more financially secure than where he came from. He excelled as navigator on the B-17 bombers, whose accuracy hastened the end of World War II. He later became a deeply respected analytic forecaster at General Electric's headquarters in New York City. He retired as a distinguished economics professor at what is now Thunderbird School of Global Management.

So, here was this nearly genius, high-capacity, driven man living his entire life with a fear he'll fall behind and return to the poverty of the Depression.

. . . Awakening . . .

Parents can unwittingly pass their fear on to their children. It teaches them to perform instead of trust.

Later, I discovered his intelligence reached well beyond his wisdom. He thought intelligence and more education alone would solve the world's problems. I wonder if many extremely intelligent people fail to learn great wisdom because they lack the humility demanded to receive it.

I would rebel against his strict demands and his inability to affirm. His approach would allow him to rarely enjoy who his son actually is—a moderately intelligent dreamer, who loves wistfulness, humor, kindness, affection, affirmation, and talking late into the night. I would become student body president and an all-state pitcher. I would date the homecoming queen. But it was not the "right" success for him. It would not translate into a law degree from Stanford. I spent too many adolescent years resenting and missing out on enjoying him because he refused to value or affirm who I actually was. He taught me a lifetime of doubting the value of the particular way I was fashioned.

I may have rejected many of his values, but I inherited most of his prideful fear. Kids from the Depression hated watching their parents be in need of handouts. Dad would not let anyone help him. If someone gave a gift or did a favor, he would quickly try to even the score or surpass it. I'm convinced this transferred fear kept me from letting others in—to see my pain, my weaknesses, my hidden brokenness, and my self-destructive choices.

Later, my dad and I would both grow up. He became an outstanding grandfather. We grew to enjoy each other with deep and tender affection. He would carry his claim of atheism to the grave. He would continue to mock every mention of God, but learned to give my family a pass. He would kindly sit by our non-aluminum tree on Christmas mornings and watch impractical gifts being exchanged, without snide comment. In his last few years on this earth he would say to me, "John, you've done so much good in your chosen profession. I've watched how you parent your children and love your wife. You're living this life very well. I'm very proud of you, son. I love you very much."

Not every son gets that blessing. I'm grateful. I wish he could see my children and their own children. He'd be deeply proud of how his name is being lived out in them.

I love my father so much. I'm deeply proud he was my father.

Jesus whispered,

John, this trust of Me you've risked—it has been clumsy and sporadic, but real. I have inhabited it completely. But you will continue to be haunted by patterns you thought you'd someday be freed of. Some of these historic illnesses of your family line may follow you until you leave this earth. But your choice to learn to trust Me will protect your family and their families beyond what you can understand now. I know. I've been up ahead. The legacy is being reformed. It fills My heart with joy and My eyes with tears telling you this.

I too have loved your dad. You can't yet have any idea what transactions people make in their hearts they cannot bring themselves to tell others. Sometimes even Mensa atheists.

1967

MY DAD GOT a big promotion in Phoenix. So, the movers came and packed us up. I still remember; we left Upland on June 24th. And my entire world began to grow smaller and smaller in the side view mirror of our Chevy Nova. I was in the back, sitting between our dog and a caged, medicated cat. The after-manufacturer air conditioner stopped blowing before we hit Blythe. Our headlights went out shortly after Quartzite. In the car, there was only shocked silence—except for the noise of the highway from our fully opened windows. One of them had my t-shirt taped and flapping in front of it. We soaked it in water back in Blythe. It now formed the centerpiece in our hopes for survival. We must've looked like a scene from *The Grapes of Wrath*. Eventually, we stumbled into our new city, feeling as though we'd driven a covered wagon through the outskirts of hell. It was ten in the evening and still over one hundred degrees. I already hated every single thing about Phoenix. I couldn't believe my father would take us from all we'd known and bring us there to die… I clearly expressed this to him upon our arrival.

All this changed in a few weeks, when I met Jim Adams. He lived three houses down. He owned a yellow Telecaster guitar and played songs I'd never heard before! He was my introduction to music and all things cool. Half the girls in our neighborhood had a crush on Jim. It was summer and he was bored of playing rock and roll all day by himself. He persuaded me to take up drums. Promising my parents good grades, I convinced them to buy me a set. Although they were purchased at a pawn shop, the snare was a Slingerland and the cymbals were Zildjian. I had, in one purchase, gone from new kid to cool new kid. By the fall, we'd formed a band. We named ourselves Metallic Wax. We now needed to find other musicians worthy of such a moniker. Within several weeks we were joined by Bob Harper on bass and Mark Finezza on rhythm guitar. By the spring of '68, we were one of the better new groups in our surrounding three-block area.

Like kids in open garages all over America, we were learning to make music. I think I'd trade my car and most of my clothing to experience again what that must have been like. I only remember wanting to play all night, working on a song over and over until it worked. It's a moment mediocre garage bands have in common with The Spencer Davis Group, Santana, and Miles Davis.

We played a couple of birthday parties and were promised money for one gig, which later got canceled. By March, Metallic Wax had gone the way of Strawberry Alarm Clock. We disbanded. Sports, girls, and our general lack of talent appeared to be our undoing.

But now I had music. I would live with a soundtrack running in the background nearly every waking moment. I would create internal playlists, guiding me through breakups and moments of anticipated greatness. In the fall of 1975, in Tucson, I was limping from a breakup with a girl I thought I'd marry. Neil Young's "Cortez the Killer" mixed with the wind as I wandered the desert, searching for the voice of some higher power.

Music became the way I would later communicate my life with

Jesus. My most intimate, honest, and vulnerable moments are spent out in neighborhoods, on beaches, or in cars, alone, making up lyrics and tunes to God. Nothing is more sacred to me.

My formal attempts at sitting and talking to God can feel forced and contrived, often degenerating into what I imagine God might want me to say, in a voice and patter even I don't trust. But when I sing to God, counting on the tune and words to find their way, I am as authentically John as I can be. It usually starts off-key and faltering but often moves into a place with God I can find in no other way. I'm trusting God to give me a song so I can stay in the moment long enough to trust Him with me.

I wonder in heaven if we'll get to see scenes we never captured down here. I'd sure like to see the four of us, playing loud and gritty rock and roll, while neighbor kids stop and stare, in awe.

John, I've got several clips of you rehearsing in Finneza's garage. Maybe I should keep looking through the archives. I haven't seen any yet where the neighborhood kids are "staring in awe."

Sorry. I couldn't help Myself.

1967

I FOUND IT in a still unpacked box in the garage. It had made it from Upland, California to our new home in Phoenix. My mom and dad's reel-to-reel tape recorder. They bought it in the late '50s, so they could exchange tape recordings with my mom's parents in Allentown, Pennsylvania as a means of keeping in touch. The concept never really worked for us. Grandpa was nearly ninety. He didn't understand technology. Thinking it was a phone, he replied and interacted with every recorded voice. He'd tell stories and yammer away about his childhood. He was born before they harnessed electricity, for crying out loud! I'm sure if I make it to be ninety years old, I'll be yammering at some new form of confusing communication too.

The reel-to-reel had been quietly waiting to be found by me at this perfect moment in my life. I had met no friends yet in Phoenix. It was June in this God-forsaken land. And much too hot to go out; day or night. Flying cockroaches, giant beetles, ticks the size of raisins, and nearly deafening, locust-like cicadas ruled this land. They were all Old Testament plague-like creatures. Even the mockingbirds were unusually angry. And why wouldn't they be? Mockingbirds were not created for one hundred and seventeen degrees.

I carried the tape recorder to my room. It was a gloriously heavy and oversized machine; turquoise and speckled white like the booths in Vince's, an Italian restaurant back in California. I clicked open the two metal clasps separating the lid from what would soon change my life.

I disliked this machine every time we used to bring it out to record something for my grandparents because it meant I would have to be quiet and then polite when called upon. But now this machine would free me to be loud and irreverent, waiting for no one to call on me. In a side pouch were half a dozen tapes; some of the only recordings left in existence of voices from Allentown. Before two weeks were out, I'll have taped over all of them. (An entire trove of Lynch family-line history erased without a moment's thought.)

From early on, I acted stuff out. Many kids do. But I got wonderfully lost in the moment. I can remember, at an early age, overhearing a friend of my mom's as we walked through a department store—"Your son, he's uh, an unusual boy. He acts things out as though others are with him." My dad didn't have room for such frivolous activity. Not when a boy could be working with an abacus or something useful of the sort. But I think my mom had always been proud of my "acting."

So, here I was now, from dawn to bedtime, recording everything I could imagine. I didn't sleep much, instead, laying in bed with my hands behind my head, organizing bits for morning's shows. I'd never really heard myself recorded before. But from that first time, I couldn't get enough of my voice! I spent hundreds of hours that summer, recording, re-recording, and editing over re-recordings. It was dreamlike.

Five-second snippets, barber episodes with scissor sound effects, "call-in" shows, "on the street" reporting, comedy club routines, recurring characters, all with my first vague attempts at accents and dialects. I made commercials for products that would never exist. Most often, I was a banquet speaker, with silverware and glasses clinking during my speeches. I gave addresses to the Kiwanis Club, confidently presenting nuanced ideas with little touch to reality. All just because I liked the way the words sounded together. I seemed so funny and talented to myself. I was learning my voice. Cadence, pace, tenor. How to walk into and out of a thought. How to understate some phrases and give drawn-out rhythm to others. I would later learn the distinction between a technical and a method actor. I am clearly the latter—and always was.

In general, technical actors systematically layer in certain motions, vocal nuances, and distinguishing mannerisms, and practice them until they become second nature. Method actors, on the other hand, find the emotional motivation of the character, and then search to discover that within themselves. While they too attend to the physical and vocal descriptions of the character, their greatest intention is to stay consistently in the heart motivation of the character they're portraying. That was me. When I was acting in those early days, I was lost in the moment, and those moments meant everything to me. I dreaded the day when school would start again and my time alone in my recording studio would be forced into competition with other humans and homework.

I had two influences in particular from '67-'69. First, there was Jonathan Winters who had his own show on CBS. Each week there was a segment allowing him to randomly "re-describe" everyday items thrown on stage from the audience. It was absolutely spellbinding. He had no net. I felt afraid for him sometimes, not sure how he'd make it home from certain bits. He was so different from other comics who pandered in silly gimmicks, mother-in-law jokes, and airline food. Winters was an unpredictable genius.

Later, Woody Allen's writings would give me permission to put hat blocking and mackerel into the same sentence. I wouldn't make it to Woodstock in 1969. But Jimmy Hendrix wouldn't get to make pretend addresses to the Kiwanis Club.

. . . Awakening . . .

All of us are given our unique "sweet spots";
talents that bring immense joy to us, but seem to
offer little redemptive value. It is great maturity
and freedom to not demand that everything have

a "spiritual" vocabulary for it to be immensely God-centered. Like a lead break in a Christian worship song, it all matters to God. All of it.

. . . .

1967

MY BROTHER DIDN'T join us in Phoenix until later in the summer. He'd been working as a counselor at a Boy Scout camp.

Looking back, how do I tell you about my brother Jim?

He was an all-district tennis player, an Eagle Scout, part of the Order of the Arrow. He was my big brother—good, kind, and deeply respected. He was my magnificent protector when my humor got me into trouble with older kids.

Then something happened none of us saw coming. He was sent home from camp early. We thought he'd maybe caught a bad case of flu. But upon his return, we quickly discovered something was very, very wrong. Something had snapped inside my brother. He had become mentally ill, deeply psychotic. He was suddenly hallucinating, speaking to himself, and had ongoing conversations with others who didn't exist. This truly great human would now become part of the best and worst mental health facilities all over the country. My tenderhearted brother would now undergo experimental drugs, shock therapy, and the terrifying life away from his home—locked up with others as tormented as him. Like every other family who has ever faced this, we had no idea what to do. That first summer, hoping I could shock him out of his stupor, I actually slugged him in the face. It only scared and confused him more. I still remember him looking shocked, dazed, and hurt. "John, why did you do that?" His rapid decline radically changed our family. We would never be the same.

Since that summer, over forty-five years ago, I've felt like a ticking time bomb, wondering when the same will happen to me. When I get overstressed or Stacey and I get into a hard enough place, I can go there. I fear one day the people who now respect me and enjoy my humor and insight will talk around me, or more slowly, or more loudly. After all, Jim was my brother. Whatever it was came from our line.

Jim passed away several years ago. This once normal, healthy athlete learned to smoke three packs a day inside mental health facilities where nearly everyone chain-smoked. Lung cancer caught up with him. Before it was diagnosed, it had spread all over his body. Within six months my brother was gone.

But one day, in his forties, God worked through the hazy slits in the blinds. My brother allowed in light. I was sitting with him in a restaurant one afternoon, embarrassed by his bursts of loud, inappropriate, crazy talk. On this particular occasion, for a reason I didn't yet know, I didn't try to quiet him down. Instead, I said, "Jim, there is a place, a land, where no one is mentally ill. My brother, there, in that place, you will be as sharp and awake as any other person." He leaned forward and whispered with lucidity I'd not seen for decades, "Where is this place, John?"

Sitting there over the next hour in that restaurant, I told him nearly everything I knew of Jesus. He asked, "John, how do I get there?" That day he trusted Jesus, and then patiently waited for the day He would take Jim to the land where his mind would work again.

. . . Awakening . . .

Not all the magnificent heroes get revealed in this lifetime. Some are trapped in bewildering chaos and illness they did not cause. This too is why Jesus came.

. . . .

On My Worst Day

1968

ARLENE ELLIS WAS another girl in the crowd. Freshman year she wore braces. But suddenly, on the first day of school in 1968, in Spanish class at Washington High School, I could not stop looking at her.

Must-act-now. Must-become-boyfriend-now!

I'd dated several girls before, but this was the first time I would realize I was no longer a kid. Several evenings later I risked what seemed my entire existence to call her. *This can go so wrong on so many levels. I might become a source of nearly legendary mocking and derision if I screw this up and word gets out. I've never risked anything like this.*

Everything had to be exactly right for this call. First, I had to find a window of time when my parents weren't home, so I could have the run of the family phone and adjoining pacing areas. I'd written out a script of what I'd say, with alternate sections depending upon her responses. Then, minutes before the call, a clumsy script rehearsal and a final edit. I had a song selected to play in the background.

If there is a god out there, I promise right now to devote my life to feeding lepers in Nepal, or whatever you'd like, if you'll just cause her to hear me out when I call. I'm willing to follow any god out there who can make this happen. Do you hear me, gods? I'm asking only for this one thing!

I was nearly dry heaving, I was so nervous. I continually shoved back the blinding anxiety and the utter sense of my universal inadequacy. I dialed all but the final number and hung up several times. I feared the first thing she'd hear would be the sound of me clearing my throat. I feared she wouldn't recognize my name.

I dialed. I heard the phone ring on her end. She answered. She sounded not unhappy that I had called. Somewhere amid my prepared sounding patter, I did manage to slip in that it would be nice to "go get a soda together sometime or something… um, like to talk over the Spanish assignments." She said she'd "like that."

Did you hear that? She said she'd "like that"!

Now, I just had to get out of the conversation without swearing or sneezing into the phone. I stumbled off the call like a blindfolded man maneuvering over a gauntlet of flaming furniture.

I hung up. I was intact! *She and I will be drinking a soda at the same table sometime in the near future. I did it! I am not a loser!* I fist-pumped my way around the house for the next few minutes, shouting and doing something approximating dance.

In that short, clipped conversation, I became a different person. Over the next several years I would live with a confidence and sense of bearing I had not known before. We would now begin to tell our lives to each other on that phone, for hours, almost every evening. I soon realized I had the capacity to give and receive love. I was being taught to articulately express affection and affirmation because I needed to find exact words to convey the depth of what I was experiencing. Those first two years were some of the most innocent, playful, and winsome days of the first half of my life. I would not know love like this until I was introduced to Stacey Marie Pilger. By then I would be almost mature enough to begin to understand what to do with it. Jesus said,

So, that promise about devoting your life to whoever could pull it off? Well, it wasn't Zeus. I should mention, for the record, you won't make good on your promise. You will ignore many more such promises before we get it right. I've never held you to them. But you are learning incredible truth these days. You are learning to believe love is indescribably powerful—that it transcends all else. Later, your hungering for a love which refuses to leave when others' loves do will draw you inexorably to Me. In the meantime, enjoy. You will spend a lot of money at expensive ice cream shoppes and movie theaters. But you will learn you are lovable—that someone wants to be with you. You will learn you have much love to give and unique ways of expressing it.

When there is no other conflicting issue on the table, I will always defer to giving you the best experiences of joy available. I'm not who you have pegged Me. I have loved you completely and perfectly from before the world began.

In the meanwhile, know this: nearly every high school guy resents and admires you for calling her first. Well played, young man, well played.

On My Worst Day

1969

PYRACANTHA IS NEARLY irrefutable proof of the existence of Satan. I believe it to be his personal plant of choice. In even the harshest climates it steadily matures into a sticker-hedge of death. I'm almost certain, as a boy, I witnessed a neighbor's dachshund chasing a ball into the pyracantha... and never coming out. A tiny yelp and then eerie silence. Two hedges of it came with our Phoenix home purchase. Front yard and back. Picture green barbed wire, with inedible red berries.

Trimming it was part of my particular list of "chores." Chores were at the center of the tension between my father and me during high school. He thought I should do them. I felt strongly I should not.

Especially during summer. I thought I should not be asked to do anything during summer break but stay out long after the streetlights came on.

I was to pick up the dog poop, clean the pool, make my bed, wash the car, mow the lawn, and keep up with the ever-advancing pyracantha. Nearly every day it was the same:

Dad: "John, did you do your chores?"

John: (indistinguishable mumbling)

Dad: "Well, you're not leaving this house until they're done."

John: (louder, nearly distinguishable mumbling)

And so it went. My halfhearted keeping of chores, after enough nagging and threats.

One June morning, this all changed. Before he walked out the door for work, he found me. I was doing nothing, preparing for an entire day of doing nearly nothing.

He was wearing black dress slacks, a starched white shirt, and a red tie, held to his shirt with a clip.

"John, I don't tell you enough how much I care about you. You bring a lot of life and laughter to our home. Your mom and I are so proud of you. Do you know that?" Then he headed to the door, turning back to say, "If you want, when I get home, we could play some catch."

Then he was off. So were my plans for the rest of the day. I still don't know what happened. Did he take a parenting class the evening before? Regardless, almost involuntarily, I walked to our shed and pulled out our hedge trimmers. They were rusted and jammed. I had no gloves. I walked out into the Phoenix summer heat to tackle the hellish pyracantha.

I dug deep into that spreading vine of death. I reshaped that ignored mass of thorns into something almost resembling a manicured hedge. It took me almost all day. I didn't care. I don't think I'd ever worked so hard. My hands were blistered from the antique hedge trimmer and my arms were bleeding from picking up thorn-covered vines formed during the Hoover administration. I took garbage can after garbage can to the alley and mowed up the last scraps I couldn't get by hand.

I was in my bedroom when I heard his '62 Chevy station wagon turn into the carport. Mom greeted him at the door. "Jim, you have to come and see what John did today!" Through the mostly closed blinds on my bedroom window, I watched him walk out to inspect what I'd done.

Then, the reason I had canceled a summer day with buddies. He smiled. I rarely got to see that smile. He was beaming. He was proud of his son. I was getting to be the son he described to me before he left for work.

A rebellious high school kid turned friend in one interchange. Though my dad didn't have God as his motivation, something about being formed in the very image of God caused him to affirm and bless a son who less than deserved it. And that son found himself wanting to bring great joy to his father.

. . . Awakening . . .

The motivation of grace will always bear greater fruit than the coercion of demand.

. . . .

On My Worst Day

1970

NO ONE IN the Lynch family tree knew how to talk about stuff. My immediate family was no different. Many households in the '60s and '70s didn't navigate communication well.

Later in life, I would learn that when a kid faces trauma and doesn't have a family to process it with, they will have no choice but to interpret their own version of the details of that event. And kids are lousy historians. So, if the untruths they tell themselves about what they saw don't get challenged, they can become ingrained. Then, as they move into adulthood, they form defense systems they don't even realize they're carrying. They just know something's not right by the way others close to them get hurt or pull away.

My mom had Type 1 diabetes—an intense form of a potentially devastating, life-long disease. She was diagnosed while in the seventh grade. It would eventually take her life. People with diabetes don't produce insulin, which modulates blood-sugar levels in the body. My mom usually erred on too little insulin. At first, she'd get dopey, like one who'd had too much to drink. By that point, she'd uncharacteristically become belligerent, no longer allowing anyone to help her. Then she'd become incoherent. Eventually, unaided, she'd enter into a diabetic coma.

Back in the '70s, managing this disease was mostly guesswork. Today, there are pumps and monitors and real-time read-outs of your exact insulin numbers.

One particular spring day of that year, I was dropped off at home after baseball practice. I walked into our house. I opened the breezeway door. "Hey, Mom." No answer. Her car was in the driveway. "Hey, Mom, I'm home!" I began walking through the house. Something was not right. I could see through the sliding glass door, she wasn't out back. "Hey, Mom. Where are you?" I walked into her bedroom to find her passed out on the floor, with the phone receiver in her hand on her chest. I had no idea what to do. I tried to shake her awake. I yelled at her. I tried to physically resuscitate her, but I didn't know what I was doing. Was she dead?! I called for an ambulance. Paramedics were soon hovering over my mom, inserting needles, and asking me a series of questions I didn't know the answers to. She was whisked away on a gurney. It's all a chaotic blur. Sirens howled down my street. People I'd never seen before were out front, gawking into our picture window.

I called my dad at work. Pacing the house, I was involuntarily carrying a horror too big for me. I was pulling emotions and fear into me that would stay.

I have no memory of when Mom and Dad returned from the hospital. What I do remember is what was not said. "How are you doing, John? You've been through a lot. Do you want to talk about it?" We Lynchs didn't do that. We just got past the event. My dad innately taught us to deal with our pain in private. That's what self-reliant children of the Great Depression did. It's what we did with tragedy. Forgiveness and affirmation—well, we didn't do those.

I wasn't told anything about what they discovered at the hospital that day. I guess they thought they could protect me by keeping me shut out. They couldn't have protected me less. That scene would replay itself nearly a dozen times in my junior and senior years of baseball practices.

Only later in life did I discover I was irrationally guarding myself from ever again experiencing defenselessness. I became hypervigilant to events that even hinted at danger. Like a background loop, my own voice warned me: *Bad things, shocking things, can happen at any moment. And there is no one to feel it with you or talk it through. Just be on guard. Always. When it happens again, block it out. Then stuff it away.*

Even still, I will move your water glass if I think it's too close to the edge. Even if I'm in your home! Just the thought of the potential panic and chaos of it falling is enough for me to grant myself permission to take over control of your water glass. Geesh.

I imagine Jesus saying,

> *I so did not want you to have to see those scenes. She never wanted to put you in those scary spots. She loved you so. But she could not protect herself from how this disease played out in her. And you would've chosen no one else to find her but you. She wanted to talk to you about it. She just didn't know how. This is life in a fallen world. It breaks My heart for you. But without allowing certain results of the Fall to play out, humanity never makes it to being born again, to being found.*
>
> *John, you will need to borrow My security for the rest of your life. It is yours for the taking. You have the full capacity to experience My strength and security. You have the capacity to experience fearlessness, even in frightening situations. I have seen all the events coming—even that morning in 1979—it has been in you all along. Meshed amidst a wonderful life, will be some*

very hard moments. I will stand with you, over you, through you, in front of you, behind you, surrounding you, and above you. Resting in this will begin to heal and free you, My friend. I love you, if possible, even more because of your fragility. If love is largely expressed in meeting your deepest needs, then I get to love you more.

1971

THE MOMENT I first saw Koufax I wanted to be a great pitcher. I never worked at anything as hard. I gave up all other sports by my junior year and concentrated on whatever I could do to become an all-state pitcher and help Washington High win a state title. In the off-season, I ran up mountains and lifted weights. Most free moments I rolled a ten-pound weight, attached with rope to a stick, up and down, to strengthen the muscles in my pitching hand. My parents allowed me to build a mound in our backyard. I cemented two beams sixty feet and six inches away and hung a mattress between them. I pitched thousands of baseballs into the square I had drawn on it. I can still hear the thud of a fastball hitting that thrift-store mattress.

Spring of 1971 surpassed even my dreams.

In my first six games, I threw two no-hitters, a one-hitter, a two-hitter, and two three-hitters. I was striking out two batters an inning! As a lefthander, I was averaging a pickoff a game. I dreamed about setting up a hitter with a high, inside fastball and punching him out with a low and away curve that would buckle his knees. I copied what I'd watched Koufax do all those years—with his same high leg kick.

One June morning, I was reading the sports page and I turned to the feature article titled, "The Arizona All-State Baseball Team." I searched for my name… There it was.

"John Lynch, left-handed pitcher. Washington High School."

My mom walked through the neighborhood with scissors to capture as many copies of the article as possible. Life felt about perfect that day…

But, when you're dreaming a dream, you often don't see past the moment of its realization. You see it happening and imagine all manner of stupendous good following it. But it doesn't always work like that. Even dreams coming true often carry an ugly asterisk next to them.

The Arizona all-state game in 1971 was played at the Cleveland Indians' spring-training stadium. In the rows behind home plate were dozens of scouts with speed guns monitoring everything in front of them. I pitched second for the North team and didn't allow a hit over my two innings, hoping I'd done enough for someone to draft me.

After the game, a scout for the Giants found me. "John, that was a mighty fine performance out there tonight. I've got to talk to some folks upstairs, but I think we're going to take you in the draft next month."

I stood there frozen, with my dad, some friends, and a scout for the San Francisco Giants! It seemed too good to be true.

It was…

He ended with the words, "All right, John Pierson, keep your nose clean. You'll hear from us." John Pierson?

The scout had mistaken me for John Pierson, my teammate from Washington High, who had also played in the game. The John Pierson who was once a close friend. The John Pierson who had recently stolen away my girlfriend.

That John Pierson.

By reflex, I got out the words, "Um, I'm not John Pierson. I'm John Lynch."

"Oh, sorry. Could you point out John Pierson to me?"

I did.

As my friends found excuses to leave at that moment, my dad and I began to make our way out from under the lights and into the dark neighborhoods where our car was parked. Nothing was spoken. But another layer of shame got added to the story, which begins with the words, "Lynch, there is something uniquely and particularly wrong with you."

For the rest of my life, I have watched many versions of that story get played out. It kicks the wind out of you. If you know God, it can twist your picture of Him.

As long as I believed God's goal for my life should be painless and smooth, with only happy endings, I lived in a cognitive dissonance, which would make me pull back and protect myself. I slipped into dangerous thinking that if He's good and powerful, our lives should be smoother and less messy than others. Bad guys should lose more often. Good guys, with a killer curve and a dream, should most often win. Sometimes it works that way. Often it does not. Not yet.

God apparently allows some of the pain of a fallen world to get through to us—believer or not. It's what He does with the pain and bad endings that ultimately proves His love and goodness. If He is able to take all of the twisted mess that finds us and is somehow able to turn it all into our good, that would be something very amazing indeed. For all the accusation He has promised too much, this is exactly what He says He is doing. "I will cause all things to work together for good" …for the likes of us.

That night at the all-state game made no sense to me. *How can something I worked this hard for end up more painful than having never tried anything at all?*

His answer to this question would come decades after this game, only after I'd trusted Him with the answer.

John, I watch how hard you try to continue to draw near to Me, even as I allow things into your life which utterly exasperate you. You're clinging to the belief that I am fully for you, and care more about you than you do. Then something happens which seems to undermine it all... I know. I watch. It deeply hurts Me to watch you experience such disappointment and a broken heart. You might try to let Me off the hook by reasoning I'm not fully in control of your world. Such thinking might maintain a measure of your affection for Me—like giving a pass for a grandfather who loves you but can't always remember your name. But this lie will ultimately ruin our relationship. I am fully in control of your world. There is nothing that happens, doesn't happen, refused, or delayed without Me seeing it, or allowing it. I am in control of your life. And I love you more than you love you. My character cannot and will not do wrong. I take whatever your race has brought on, and I redeem, refashion, and rework it all into beauty beyond anything you could have possibly imagined. All things. Horrible things. Evil things. Chronic things. I decide what is allowed through and what it will accomplish. I decide what needs to be refashioned. But mostly I stand in the arena, when you cannot stand, defending you and protecting you. I do not lecture; I do not mock. What I do is love you, no matter how angry you are at Me, no matter what you imagine in your heart about Me. I enter into your pain more deeply than even you. This I can do. This I will always do. Until we are home together in the land where tears cease.

1972

IT WAS ALWAYS about playing hard and coming home tired with enough memories of glory to sustain our dreams. It was always about laughing hard and having a great adventure. When we were done with the day, we'd lie on our backs in the cool grass, with our arms folded behind our heads, staring at clouds, and retelling to each other a version of a game much better than what actually happened. In my neighborhood, nobody talked about discipline or taking it seriously. But we played harder, enjoyed it more, and had each other's backs better than any organized team we would ever play on after it.

That's why it hurt so badly to get trashed by a coach for enjoying it so much when I got to college.

I had scholarships to other schools after high school, but Arlene Ellis chose Arizona State University. So, without a scholarship and way in over my head, I continued my boyhood dreams at ASU, under Coach Bobby Winkles. He was the man! A legendary backwoods, tobacco-spitting, old-school coach, he had turned Arizona State from nearly intramural baseball to a program yearly competing for an NCAA national championship.

He liked me. He appreciated my passion and love of the game. He started me in center field one practice game. He rarely put pitchers in other positions. I hit the first pitch from Dale Hrovat over the center field fence at Goodwin Stadium! Next inning, I misplayed a fly ball and was back to pitching. But still! I don't think I ever enjoyed playing for a coach as much.

But in those days, the freshmen were coached primarily by the assistant coach. He enjoyed me not much at all.

I was surrounded by nationally recruited, blue-chip, flame-throwing sensations; most would go on to long major-league careers. I was now a junk-throwing local kid with a damaged shoulder and a memory of a fastball. I shouldn't have tried to hang on. But I wasn't ready to leave the game. I'd thrown some surprisingly good winter ball stints in relief. I still thought I'd make it back and would get drafted in late rounds.

But mostly, baseball was still fun to me. Warming up is nearly every ballplayer's favorite part of the sport. The fifteen minutes before drills, batting practice, fielding, and intersquad games. It was our refuge—from schoolwork, from responsibility, from the looming seriousness of life.

Each of us had warmed up thousands of times in ball fields all over the country. We knew that ball-hitting-glove sound like our own voices. It was therapy and a theme park all at once. This was where the best humor came out. We'd mock each other. We'd work on our invented knuckleballs. (All college ballplayers think they can throw a knuckleball). We'd turn our gloves inside out. We chewed tobacco and sang jingles from commercials. We'd talk trash about each other's girlfriends. And, in a raw and clumsy way, we learned to have each other's backs. We knew when to get serious. All of us did. But as time-honored as any unwritten baseball rule, screwing around while getting loose has always been near the top.

At least I thought so.

In one of our routine team meetings, sitting on the grass in the outfield, the assistant coach wanted to talk about "discipline and taking things seriously." He chose me as the scapegoat to make his point. He tore me apart in front of my friends and fellow ballplayers.

"Lynch, you think you're so damned funny. You think everything's a joke. You know how to get others to screw around until my good players forget why we brought them here. Lynch, you're like a cancer to a team. Did you all hear me? Players like Lynch are a cancer. They poison the water and others don't even notice it. Well, that's not the way we won a national championship when I played first base here, and it's not the way we're going to play ball now, dammit! So, Lynch, you decide what you are—a ballplayer or a comedian... All right, everyone, get to work."

It's a uniquely horrible feeling to be shamed as an athlete. Something in your masculinity, in your very person, gets diminished. The respect and hard-earned trust between ballplayers is experienced at every level. We were used to getting called out for not running hard on an infield pop-up. But none of us were prepared to have our personhood attacked. This coach knew what he was doing. He was ostracizing me from the rest of the team. Hanging out with me would risk becoming this coach's next target.

That was the last day I would enjoy playing baseball. I would leave the game forever three weeks later.

John, I formed you to encourage community—to affirm, bless, enjoy, and bring out the best in others. When you run up against an insecure person who can coach only by threatening and belittling, your motive will always be misunderstood. And you will get hurt.

This moment will help develop a conviction you will teach

for the rest of your life; people work best and hardest in a place where they know they are valued.

I am going to surround you with some strong friends, who will protect you as you model and teach this way of life.

None of this will help you much for about twenty years. What happened today will wound you. You will have no one to protect you. Until this moment, you have respected and obeyed even bad authority. But this will change you. It will give you increasing permission to mistrust all authority. You are about to enter a brutally hard time of your life.

I'm here. One day, you'll understand I suffered under insecure authority which ultimately tried to destroy one who would threaten it with good. You're in good company today. You just don't know it yet. By the way, that coach, he knows he's wrong. He will go home after today's practice and sit in front of a television set and know he's wrong. You'll be teaching this way of life to his sons and daughters. Hold on, kid.

. . . Awakening . . .

In an environment of law, every motive is suspect. In an environment of grace, good motive is presumed.

, , , , , , , , , ,

October, 1972

WE WERE OUT for dinner one evening, Arlene and I. Recently, things had not been going well with us. But nothing had prepared me for the words she said to me that night...

"John, I think we should break up."

She had seen enough. She had known me for six years. We'd been together almost every day. She loved me and deeply enjoyed me. But I was too much work. I had not learned how to be secure dating this uncommonly beautiful girl. She had grown weary of defending herself. My insecurity and shame were now disrupting my world at its very core.

How hard it must have been for her to prepare to say those words! How long did she know and not tell me, afraid of hurting me? In the moment, I was not mature enough to tell her how brave she was.

Everything that happened next was a frantic blur. I paid the check before our meal arrived and drove her home in the rain. Neither of us spoke a word. There was only the sound of windshield wipers, mocking me. I dropped her off and stared at her one more time before she walked out of my sight.

I drove wildly back to the fraternity. My best friend was not in his room. I banged on his door like a deranged man, yelling at the top of my lungs. Then, in my shiny white shoes and dress slacks, I ran through the streets of Tempe, moaning out loud, "This time it is really over."

As long as she was in my world, I could make sense of life. She was not only a girlfriend. Her affirmation and smile were how I knew who I was. Now suddenly I was alone. Another thick layer of shame was being formed on that run. To have someone know me up close for a long, long time, for that person to know the deepest, most real truths about me, to know my dreams, my secrets, my weaknesses, and then choose to no longer be with me, to not be enough for that person. *Where do I go? What do I do with the rest of this life? Who is built to withstand such pain?*

I discovered myself in a park, miles away, panting and drenched.

. . . Awakening . . .

Rejection can tempt me to spend the rest of my life proving I'm worth loving. But it will never convince me.

. . . .

The most darkness-defying risk a human can take is to believe, even in the moment, this is true: In my freshly proven shame and sense of failure, I want to turn away from it. But to do so is to deny the reason Jesus went to the cross.

On my worst day, I am: adored, enjoyed, clean, righteous, absolutely forgiven, new, acceptable, complete, chosen, able, intimately loved, smiled upon, planned for, protected, continually thought about, cared for, comforted, understood, known completely; given all mercy and compassion; guarded, matured, bragged on, defended, valued, esteemed, held, hugged and caressed, kissed, heard, honored, in unity with, favored, enough, on time, lacking nothing, directed, guided continually, never failed, waited for, anticipated, part of, belonging, never alone, praised, secure, safe, believed, appreciated; given all grace, all patience; at peace with, pure, shining, precious, cried over, grieved with, strengthened, emboldened, drawn kindly to repentance, relaxed with, never on trial, never frowned at, never hit with a two-by-four, at rest in, receiving complete access, given gifts, given dreams, given new dreams, continually healed, nurtured, carried, never mocked, never punished; most of my humor enjoyed, not behind, not outside, given endless affection.

It doesn't always much feel like it in the moment. This is the depth of His love, whether you or I feel we deserve it or not. "Deserve" has long ago left the building.

On My Worst Day

1973

THE COMBINATION OF Arlene leaving and my baseball career ending did me in. Within a few months, my clothing style changed. I grew my hair long and I moved out of the fraternity. Without debate, I gave myself permission to live a life I'd previously never considered. I spent more time with an older friend, who introduced me to a countercultural lifestyle. I started eating tofu and lentil beans with curry. Soon, I was trying out transcendental meditation and studying the teachings of Baba Ram Dass. I checked out nearly every hip manner of spirituality I could locate. I smoked pot daily and would soon aggressively plow my way through all manner of psychedelic drugs. I read Carlos Castaneda, Richard Brautigan, Kurt Vonnegut, and *Zen and the Art of Motorcycle Maintenance*. I tried dating girls I knew from the sororities, but my heart was not in it. They were far too much part of the "establishment" for my new thinking.

Dad had taken a promotion to General Electric headquarters in Connecticut. The next time my parents would see me, I'd present as an entirely different son. One of my strong regrets is that I forced them to react to my new directions instead of giving them the gift of walking with me through it. I did this to them over and over through the next decades. Near the end of his life, my dad told me he wished I hadn't imposed my newfound faith as a line-in-the-sand declaration. "Do you know how hard it is for your son to defiantly tell you he now believes differently than you, without ever giving you the chance to enter the conversation?"

John, you are trying to navigate life without anyone standing next to you. You are afraid of being hurt. You think you are more open-minded, but are actually closed to everything but bluffing. You are open to all manner of lies. You will try nearly everything, except Me. Tonight, as you lie in bed, I am trying to help you know I'm here. I'm not angry, I'm not disgusted. I'm waiting. This next part of this story will be horribly hard. But I promise, I will not let a minute of it be wasted. After it is all over, you will wake up and still be right on time.

1973

IN TWO SEMESTERS, I would change my major from political science, to psychology, to recreation, then English. My major at the moment was speech communication, with a minor in drama. In the theater, I discovered the vehicle I would communicate from for much of the rest of my life. In my first acting class, I discovered an uncommon ability to bring printed words alive on a stage. I discovered a professor and mentor named Dr. Witt. He was a short, rumpled, pudgy man in his fifties, with a bushy mustache and wild hair. He was an eccentric, brilliant, accomplished stage actor and director. I had been spellbound, watching him act and direct actors. In his beginning acting class, I performed a soliloquy from *Long Day's Journey into Night*. As soon as I sat down, he dramatically popped up and slithered up close to the class. He put his forefinger to his lips, tilted his head to the side, and whispered, "Shh… For a moment, try to absorb what happened. That, right there. What you just watched. That was acting! This is why I love teaching. For moments like this. Where someone with no training shows up and brings something alive and real to this stage. The rest of you dullards move from one piece of furniture to another, reciting words as from a recipe card. This young man made me believe him. He believed himself. Whatever it is he understands, the rest of you need to discover. Or your only role in the theater will be as prop-handlers in a cafetorium production of *Pippen*."

I sat there staring, realizing in that moment, this was the gift I would carry for the rest of my life. I only needed another to see it in me.

I love everything about taking on a character: the preparation, the memorization, blocking, self-directing, getting into character, and then playing it all out in front of others. No net. The audience and actors create a moment that wouldn't exist otherwise. Both are indispensable to the other.

The only movie where I've seen this truth captured is *Shakespeare in Love*. We are watching the beginning of the first-ever performance of Romeo and Juliet. It is sputtering out of the gate. The play is given up on by nearly everyone within five minutes. Then a vulnerable line is believably delivered. And a spark catches. In moments, the audience is now trying, through nodding and leaning, to call out to the actors: "We're here. We've bought in. We've got you. Run with this!

We'll catch you if you fall. Please, give us something which will help us transcend our lives. We will do our part." The actors soon find their footing. A permission from trust has been forged. Something palpable and tangible, wild and unbridled is being created that never existed before this moment. Everyone knows magic is happening, and no one will allow this spell to be broken...

I'm not really an actor, at least not in the classical sense. I just think I am comfortable being John Lynch in different outfits. I can convince you I believe I am who I am portraying. That's all it takes for an audience to buy in and allow you to take them to another place, to another way of seeing.

Theater is not only what takes place on a stage. You don't have to be an actor to pull out a memory and bring it to those who were not there. Whenever that takes place, something magical happens. It's the key to great teaching, storytelling, parenting, songwriting, or opening your heart. To take yourself back into a redemptive moment and replay it. It inspires and frees others. It's about as close as transcending into the eternal as we get down here. When you can get out of the way of your self-consciousness long enough to convince another you are there in the moment, it allows them to be transported to places they might otherwise never get to go. All of it is exceedingly life-giving.

With all the pain and ugliness of what would be coming up, I remain grateful that God used this time to teach me how to be me in front of others. I learned a craft I would get the privilege to perform the rest of my life, to one day help free others into grace.

You will never be able to quickly tell a wrench from a pair of pliers. You will never successfully work on anything electrical your entire life. But this I have given you to do. Do you know how much I enjoy watching you unwind a piece, while I sit in the audience with others, allowing Myself to be transported into the scene you create? Yes, Me. That's what love does. It trusts another to benefit from who they are. Bravo, My friend. Bravo!

On My Worst Day

1975

NO MONEY I'VE ever possessed was spent as well as the two hundred twenty-five dollars I paid for that blue 1960 Ragtop VW Bug.

I graduated from college in May. While most of my friends were transitioning into careers they'd been interning for, I pointed that car and her misfiring cylinders toward Santa Barbara. Several years before, during a spring break trip, the fuel pump in my '65 Chevy Nova went out and had to be repaired in Isla Vista, outside of Santa Barbara. I spent three days there with a friend. I drove away in love with all things beach town.

For the next several years, I lived with only what my VW could carry as I waited tables from Santa Barbara to Laguna Beach.

I developed a predictable pattern: show up in a new town, sleep in my car, find a waiter's job, move in with other waiters. I loved being the winsome new guy with stories to tell of the open road. I was made for waiting tables! You're given money for helping others enjoy their time. For a performer, that's easy money. We ate the food guests left on their plates. At a nice steak and fish house, you could score lobster, crab, and steak all evening long. Ramen during the day; surf and turf at dinner.

I stayed in each town until things got too complicated. Then I'd pack up Blue and move on.

I loved my car. I drove her long distances, mostly at night. She couldn't handle the desert during the day. I propped up the engine cover an inch or so with a fishing rod, so she wouldn't vapor lock. Her 6-volt battery spent more time dead than alive. I learned to park on slants, so later I could push her with the driver's door open, hop in, drop into second gear, lurch her into life, and head off down the road. With Jackson Browne's "For Everyman" blaring through the speakers, it was a hippie's dream.

I'd drive through the night, with her ragtop wide open, creating radio talk shows. I made up an imaginary talk show host, who'd take calls from all manner of imaginary people.

"Hello, this is Bob Abernathy. You're on the air. What's your gripe? What's your complaint?"

"Yep, Bob, thanks for the handle. I'm Floyd McCutcheon. I'm driving a big rig outta Sioux Falls, heading to Barstow on a blind flip to Chi town."

"What you carrying, Floyd?"

"Bearings, Bob. Lateral cinch bearings for farm equipment. You use 'em to modulate your flashpoint while galvanizing sheet metal into bevel housing conduits. Try torquing an aftermarket adapter without cinch bearings and you'll be pulling rivets out of your Ditch Witch like silt from a frontload grain harvester. You know what I mean, Bob?"

"So, Floyd, what's your gripe? What's your complaint?"

…There is no accent or voice I use today who didn't first call into Bob Abernathy's show.

That car taught me to love road trips, seek out diners, enjoy cow-shaped creamers, eat pie, make small talk with locals, smell night air, watch stars over me, form new dialects, and be comfortable alone, with myself, driving along, waiting to meet Everyman.

I still love all of it.

. . . Awakening . . .

God enjoys the tastes and enjoyments I cultivated in my unbelieving days. He only wants to enjoy them with me and discard the ones that hurt me.

. . . .

John, when you were forced to sell Blue for rent money back in Connecticut, I made sure she had a great final owner. An older widow in upstate New York. She saw the car sitting in front of a Chinese restaurant with a for sale sign on the front windshield. She'd driven past it every day for months. She loved that car. She used to be a hairstylist for The Yardbirds. The bass player had one the same color you repainted yours. One day she said to Me, "If that car is still there a month from now, I'm going to take it as a sign You'd like me to have it." People are throwing that kind of nonsense at Me all the time. I don't want to encourage it. Next thing I know, I'm being asked to make the sunset a certain color. Anyway, for her, I made an exception. I wanted your car to have a great last home. I'm sentimental like that. So sue Me.

For ten years she drove that beauty from her farm outside Mount Kisco into town and back. Her dogs loved the open top.

They put their paws on the back of the front seats and stuck their heads out the top of the car. The car never had a repair. I thought you should know.

1977

EARLY ON, I drove with friends to Las Vegas. Later, I got a ride with near strangers. Eventually, I hitchhiked by myself.

I still don't know why Vegas drew me. I'd been told a dozen reasons why it shouldn't have. Maybe it's because I had started going there back in the early '70s, when attractive cocktail waitresses would come to your chair at the slot machines and kindly offer you immense free shrimp cocktails.

Even the bathrooms were over the top. Every casino on the Strip had bathroom valets! They would buff shoes, light cigarettes, or whisk suit coats. I always wished I could borrow a coat, so I could get a whisking and maybe a story from one of those friendly old attendants. Each had an entire table of elegant and expensive male grooming accoutrements: witch hazel, hair sprays and gels, mouth-wash, deodorant, cologne, gum. And combs waiting in a giant cylinder of bright-blue sanitizer. It was all so completely opposite of my wooden-crate decor of madras curtains and bean bag chairs. It was so completely otherworldly for me—a flannel-shirt-wearing hippie in this sparkly-leisure-suit town.

I had the bad fortune of winning five hundred dollars the first time I went. I thought this was how Vegas worked. But, almost every trip after, through college and beyond, I would wager and eventually lose most of my money for the month. I learned in those days how to live on potato salad for weeks at a time.

My first time there was for a tournament with the Phoenix American Legion Baseball All-Stars. I was eighteen, and still wearing braces, but somehow I found myself seated at a blackjack table inside the Sahara. In those days, at a corner of each table, they provided a clear plastic bin of non-filtered cigarettes. I loved all the freebies. So I tried one. I figured it might help me look older. I ordered a Harvey Wallbanger because it's what the guy next to me was drinking. Then I put a Lucky Strike into my mouth. I didn't light it. I only wanted to look like I belonged at a place where filterless cigarettes are an anticipated choice.

Cigarettes and braces are a bad combination. The dealer could see it all happening right in front of him. I was oblivious. It was the middle of the afternoon. There was an attractive young woman, several seats away at this two-dollar table. I glanced over at her, like I was the drummer for a band playing somewhere tonight on the Strip. If she had looked over, she would have seen my braces covered and my chin wet with Lucky Strike tobacco—dripping onto my shirt.

Whenever I think I'm somebody more than I am, the dealer's words from that afternoon come back to me:

"Son, I'm going to have to ask you to put what's left of that cigarette into the ashtray. You're getting wet tobacco all over my table. And you might want to check your smile in the restroom mirror."

But on this particular day in 1977, seven years later, I was outside Wickenburg, trying to look non-threatening, hoping to catch a ride to Caesar's Palace. After about an hour, a giant Cadillac slowed past me and honked for me to get in. There were giant cattle horns on the front hood of this jet-black beauty. As I slid in, the driver smiled, tipped his giant cowboy hat, and growled in a deep, raspy Texan voice, "Howdy, young man. The name's Laramie Jordan."

Laramie Jordan. It was a stage name that stuck for him. He told me he used to have a local television show, *The Laramie Jordan Show*, back in the late '50s on KPHO. From the moment I got in until he dropped me off before disappearing into the Caesar's Palace private underground parking garage, he never stopped talking. A friendly, washed-up semi-celebrity, wanting someone to hear stories from when he ruled the airwaves.

He bought me lunch in Kingman. "Order whatever you like, young fella." He never asked anything about me. But before he dropped me off he said this:

"Young fella, you have a great time. Live it up. Don't even think about the consequences. But on the day you turn thirty, I want you to look into the mirror and take stock of who are you. You hear me, young man? Thirtieth birthday. You remember old Laramie Jordan told you to do it. All right. Time for you to get out of the car. Mama needs a new pair of snakeskin boots!"

He tipped his hat and was gone. I never saw him again.

That night, I played blackjack and drank whisky for hours and hours. I turned two hundred dollars into sixteen hundred dollars, and then back to zero dollars. I vividly remember walking out of the casino, angry with myself for not being able to stop. *What's wrong with you? Who are you? What are you going to do now? It's the thirteenth and you don't get any more money until the start of the month. How are you going to explain this back home? Why do you do this? Are you sick?*

I laid down in the grass out near the pool at the Sands casino and passed out. I awoke several hours later, sopping wet from sprinklers, which had turned on moments before. I stumbled to my feet and found my way to a road leading me out of town.

It's one thing to be a college kid going up for a weekend to Las Vegas with buddies. It's very much another to be completely alone, having lost all my money for the month, sopping wet, swearing at myself, trying to thumb a ride in the middle of the night. I had no more illusions of my imperviousness to misfortune.

I was now not that far from God.

On the day I turned thirty, I would be a believer, in seminary, sane, sober, and taking second-year Greek. And because five years earlier Laramie Jordan had told me to, I would find myself that evening, looking into the bathroom mirror, and almost involuntarily taking stock of who I am…

Thank you, Laramie Jordan.

1977

DRIVING SOUTH FROM Los Angeles, past Newport, Corona Del Mar, and Crystal Cove State Park, you'll drop into Laguna Beach. It remains transcendent, iconic, and full of indelible memories for me. Shaw's Cove, Main Beach, the Sawdust Festival, South Coast Cinemas, the Hotel Laguna, and the Surf and Sand.

At one time, the Surf and Sand was Laguna's premier destination hotel, resort, and conference facility. For decades they ran The Boardwalk Restaurant on the same property, overlooking the Coast Highway that takes you to Carlsbad and San Diego. It was the Surf and Sand's more affordable and accessible, but still exceptional, steak, grilled seafood, and fresh lobster house. I was a waiter there in 1977. I could have become a senator. But apparently, I didn't have the chops, education, vision, or anyone to direct me into such a thing. But waitering I could do. Except for the actual serving of food part. That was not a particular strength for me. But all the rest played into the best of my personality, talents, and acting abilities. It turns out, I'd been waiting to find such a platform and didn't even know it. And The Boardwalk had apparently been waiting for me.

Pat Pierson was the manager. He invited his brother, John, and me to come work there. John, if you remember, was the All-State second baseman that the Giant scout mistook me for, back in 1971. We had since become close friends.

Pat was an exceedingly good manager. He understood if you give freedom and protection for others to try out who they innately are, they will give you back their best and never want to defraud you. A bad manager, watching you like a hawk and presuming you want to steal from them, will likely get your worst, and in the end, you will probably try to steal something from them, just because. I think Pat's trust in me caused me to be myself as soon as I figured out the whole serving food part.

Every shift was a canvas to paint wildly upon. I am built for an audience. And this setting was waiting to become one. One Friday evening, after several weeks of training at The Boardwalk, I was serving a wonderful couple I had met the week before. I still don't know why I did what I'm about to tell you. I only know it felt right and I thought it might bless Pat, this couple, and nearly everyone in the restaurant. The Boardwalk had three or four large, open, airy rooms, with a bar. You could hear and see into every room.

Suddenly, I called out loudly enough for everyone to hear, "Ladies and gentlemen, your attention, please! This is my man, Walt Stevens. Would you please stand, Walt?" Walt shyly stood, having no idea what was coming next. "It's Walt's birthday today. I know he looks 75 but today, Walt turns 52." Laughter. "But seriously, I would refuse tips and I'd sleep in this restaurant's walk-in cooler, if all guests were like him and his wife, Sally. I've served many of you. And I would not sleep in the walk-in cooler for you folks. And I mean that in the kindest way." Loud laughter. "What Walt will not tell you is that since moving to Laguna eight years ago, he has volunteered to help build sets for every one of Laguna High's drama productions. In addition, these two own a clothing store down near Main Beach. They have a policy to give coats to anyone passing through Laguna, who can't afford one. Who does that? I got one when I came into town. It was a little embarrassing when we met here at the restaurant. I felt compelled to give the coat back. So far, I haven't." Much laughter. "Walt is one of the most kind, humble, and respectful people I've ever met. He's probably dying a thousand deaths as I'm doing this. Oh, and if people sing 'Happy Birthday' to him, his neck breaks out in hives." Laughter. "So, as JoAnne performs this high-danger ballet of serving these flaming Grand Marniers to the both of them," laughter, "would you please stand, and join me in applauding this really good man's life?"

The place went nuts! It was electric. The applause lasted almost a minute. Suddenly, it was like we had all been invited guests for Walt's retirement dinner. I felt, for the first time in a long time, like I was hosting something real and good. I leaned to see Pat sitting at the bar, smiling. Others got up and walked over to Walt and Sally, to congratulate them and introduce themselves. It was magical and spontaneously kinetic—the kind of stuff you tell your friends about during the week. "Hey, I was at The Boardwalk last Friday. You won't believe what happened!" Soon, others were requesting all manner of celebrations to be toasted: birthdays, anniversaries, retirements, and honeymoons. Other servers started to get in on the fun. We would maybe do a dozen a night over the weekend. It gave The Boardwalk a genuine, playful expression that reflected Laguna's eclectic, artist-town feel.

I was created to kindly, meaningfully, and nearly irreverently, affirm. There is a playful sarcasm that, in its expression, conveys powerful value and love. Not everyone will always appreciate this way I have been made. But as long as I can get away with it, this is me.

Later, I imagined Jesus speaking to me that evening.

John, that could have gone wrong in twelve different ways. But it didn't. You made Walt feel so valued. He gives a lot to this community and there hasn't always been a vehicle for him to experience much encouragement in return. Tonight, you offered that vehicle. Then you slipped back into the server's area to allow patrons to find each other. Everyone in the restaurant felt important, just getting to play and be part of such a life-giving moment. This is love, out in public. You just don't know the source of it yet. My people need to know God is playful with them like this. Bad religion has taught them that there's a chasm between religious fun and what happened this evening. Sadly, many folks are their most real selves at times like tonight and sometimes they are their most pretend at church. John, this was never supposed to happen. What happened to My Church? She was supposed to offer a healthy playfulness that would build others up just as the world searches for. Kind of like what they're getting from a pagan, dope-smoking atheist this evening. Well done, My friend. Hang in there. It won't be long now. One day you'll be doing this for My glory. I love you.

1977

AFTER ABOUT A year, I returned from waiting tables in beach towns. I was now back in Phoenix; most evenings performing melodrama parodies as part of a small theater company at an iconic western steak-house north of town. When you paid for your ticket, you received a program, with the bios of each of the actors. If you had read mine, it would have said, at some point, "John performed and was held-over as a stand-up comedian through much of 1976 at Borsodi's, a night club in Isla Vista, California." Impressive. Except it wasn't true. Never happened. I made it up.

I was twenty-four at this point. All my life I'd been told I was exceedingly funny. I always believed it. The bio should have mentioned I actually did stand-up comedy... One evening. One set. One part of one set. That's all that was needed. The evening is seared into my psyche, if only from the intensity of that spotlight trained on me. Let me try to tell it in real-time.

I'm at Yesterdays, a bar on Mill Avenue. On this particular evening, I follow local blues legend, Hans Olson. Hans is wearing an eye patch from an accident as a kid. He is dressed like an angry homeless man. An angry homeless man who combs his hair with an oil-soaked rake. He might be the scariest looking performer I've seen since a particular state fair from my childhood... I digress.

In the break, just before I go on Hans checks me over. To him, I must look like a supermarket check-out boy. He gruffly mumbles something like, "Hey, kid, this gig ain't for everyone. Don't look at the spotlight. It'll blind you. Then you're screwed." With that sage encouragement, I walk out to an audience who apparently has been alerted to *not* enjoy me. Material that had been funny to my friends for decades is met with haunting silence. Zero laughs. I cut my act short—by about two-thirds. If I hadn't voluntarily stepped off, I think the crowd would have physically removed me. I can sense torches being lit.

So, why now, two years later, would I make up such a pervasive lie about something I had failed at so badly?

Graduating from Arizona State University, many other friends had important careers waiting for them. IBM, Honeywell, television stations. And here I was, wandering around, living a gap year, before they even existed. But my gap year was heading into a gap lifetime. Friends would write to me about raises, advancements, and engagements. I was smoking dope, pretending I'd read Carlos Castaneda's books, and working as a waiter on State Street in Santa Barbara. I was so broke that when my brakes went on my VW Bug, I used the handbrake to work my way around town for months. I just had to have something more impressive to tell people. My shame hadn't told me just how far I would go not to be embarrassed.

Borsodi's was a real place. A cool, funky, hippie hangout. Nobody did comedy there—doped-up hippies don't laugh with the same focus as a beer-drinking crowd. And so John Lynch began to learn to have an alternate universe. And for it to work, nobody could come to town to visit. If someone wanted to, I told them I was down in L.A. doing some shows. For several years, Borsodi's was on every job application, every bio, and part of nearly every introduction I would make. It wasn't until I trusted Jesus that I came clean. I told my best friends, Jim and Pam Addams. They didn't have much of a response. When pressed, Pam said, "Johnny, I'm not sure we were certain whether or not you did stand-up comedy in Santa Barbara. But we didn't really care. We love you so much. And we both agree, if you weren't doing comedy, you sure could have. You're very, very funny. We believe in you." And that was that.

Amongst all the truths that came out of her response, three stand out. First, those closest to you know that you probably make crap up, because they've seen it all along. Secondly, they don't feel the need to call you out. They will wait until you are able to tell the truth about yourself, and in the meantime, they will love what you're able to give them. Third, love means seeing the best in you, maybe even over-believing in you.

I can't believe what I eventually got to do with my life—acting out Christ's love to others—is God giving me the desires of my heart. I guess the joke is kindly on me.

1978

AND GOD MADE His second entrance.

I was waiting for Him to show up again all my life. I just wasn't sure who it was. Jackson Browne sang about waiting here for Everyman. I was now desperately waiting, holding on. I didn't know it was Him I was waiting for.

Jesus.

Oh, how the very name freaked me out. Growing up with my atheist, socialist dad, Jesus was blamed for every societal weakness. All Christians were uneducated, snake-handling frauds, whose ancestors started every war.

Still, I was searching the landscape. The American Dream had now completely slipped the rails. The homecoming queen was gone. My all-state pitching hand was stained yellow from cigarettes. I lived in growing paranoia, imagining every cop knew about the bag of weed stuffed under my passenger seat.

I was now in Laguna Beach, living with a girl in an apartment on the Coast Highway. On one particular spring Saturday, we decided to see a movie. The main beach theater was playing *Oh, God!*—a simplistic comedy about God, living incognito, on earth. God was played by George Burns, a deadpan, crotchety old vaudeville actor.

He portrayed God as a cigar smoker with a dry wit and a willingness to admit He made the avocado pit too large. Something about the picture of a God willing to poke fun at Himself flipped a switch inside me.

I couldn't speak as I walked out of the theater. She asked what was wrong. I couldn't tell her. I didn't know. We walked across the street and through the lobby of a hotel, out to a balcony overlooking the Pacific Ocean. We ordered wine. It was silent for a while.

And there, right then, hope topped the horizon. For the second time in my life, I was overwhelmed with the all-encompassing presence of the God of the universe. It was consistently as strong, certain, and pure as those two minutes at age eleven.

Hold on, kid. It won't be long now.

In that moment, staring out into the setting sun, I began sobbing. In that same moment, the woman sitting across from me was probably pondering which new guy she'd now be moving in with…

1979

I WAS BACK in Phoenix, teaching high school drama and English. It had been a year since the God experience on the balcony in Laguna. Over those months, I'd gradually tried to rationalize it all as the mystical experience of emotions mixed with a movie, wine, and a sunset. The Laguna Beach girl decided to move to Phoenix with me, convinced I was over my Jesus moment. But lately, I was listening to an album a friend had given me. Keith Green was a Christian songwriter who once played piano in a band on the Sunset Strip. It was the first Christian album I'd heard which didn't sound like Muzak or funeral home music.

I started to read the Bible. I mostly read the words in red. Jesus was coming off as the coolest hippie ever! He told the crowds not to worry about how they're gonna make ends meet. Like it's all gonna work out. He said the birds don't worry about things and yet God knows when any of them fall from the sky. I discovered He knows how many hairs are on everyone's head. I wasn't sure why He wants to know this, but I was impressed. I watched Him care for the sick and walk into bars to hang out with the dregs of society.

I was at the exact place millions get to. I was becoming drawn to Jesus, but the hurdles to Him seemed insurmountable. I had too many questions, like…

1. How could this man Jesus be God? That's like saying spinach dip is a barn owl.
2. There's not enough whisky to believe God would come to earth as a baby, through a woman.
3. The resurrection is creepy, sci-fi sounding stuff. Nowhere in my world does anything like that happen.
4. How can a book this old, written by fallible humans, ever be trusted?
5. His followers, almost to a person, come off as pretentious, bluffing, superstitious kooks, who dress like they have a date with a covered wagon.
6. I'd have to give up dope. I am not giving up dope.
7. Their music makes one wish the synthesizer had never been invented.
8. I don't have the energy to bluff better behavior.
9. Christian television.
10. I will not play the fool and believe a religious opiate. I must hold out on my search for truth.

John, My boy, I don't want to rub it in. But you will, one day, have to give answers to this stuff for others like you. Again, only an observation…

1979

GOD MOMENTS WERE starting to happen more and more often now.

A friend asked me to join him to get out of town for a couple of days. He knew some lawyer friends in San Diego who would put us up. We drove in Friday evening, joining them for dinner, drinks, and several joints. These guys were well-read, brilliant, immensely funny. Eventually, the conversation got around to mocking Jesus and Christians. This had been a common default subject in my world for a long time. But for the first time, I couldn't join in. Suddenly, these lawyers seemed like the simpletons, with their tired approach of marginalizing God by mocking the most bizarre of His followers. All three noticed I wasn't taking part. My friend asked me what was going on. I thought to myself, *I can no longer mock Him.* I found myself saying, "You ever read about Him? I've been reading a Bible recently. I don't want to make fun of Him anymore. If any of what they've written is true, He was a pretty remarkable person. If you could hear yourselves, it all sounds so petty and small. Like we're mocking because we're afraid it could be true. It's like we're all afraid of something, or we'd leave it alone."

My friend was now glaring at me, knowing I'd ruined our chance at two nights in San Diego. We probably got in the car and headed back to Phoenix. I did know I had crossed a line. I was now in between worlds—no longer belonging anywhere.

John, I don't know if you can understand how profoundly beautiful it is to Me, what you did. You were defending Me. You were hurt for Me. You risked alienation to have My back. Thank you. I will not forget this evening.

1979

I WAS SITTING on my bed, listening to a Bob Dylan album. Dylan was my generation's prophet. He had been on more covers of *Rolling Stone* than any individual musician. Twenty-five minutes before, I pulled *Slow Train Coming* from its album jacket and put the turntable needle to vinyl. I had no idea what to expect. There were rumors Dylan had embraced a new faith. I listened without moving for the entire album side, crying and sighing like I might stop breathing. The needle skipped at the end for several minutes before I again realized where I was. The last song, "When He Returns," left me ruined.

Before the day was over I played both sides half a dozen times. God used Dylan to crumble my last wall. To hear him sing those words told me the old order was being swallowed up. The renegades and chain-smokers were being invited in. If Dylan could pen this love, maybe it was for me too…

The rest of the way was paperwork. My weakness was about to become unconcealed.

John, back in 1966, I had Claude Osteen's shoulder stiffen up so you could see Koufax. Today, I have timed Bob Dylan's journey to meet yours in this cold room on Thirty-sixth Street, north of Thomas. I put this all together before the world began. I love you this much. I know how your heart works; I knew exactly the timing for this regeneration. I promised you it would not be much longer. You will read The Great Divorce *by Lewis and watch* Jesus of Nazareth *early this Christmas season. Several more of your students will talk with you about Me. A total stranger will stop you in a mall and tell you about Me. You will be surprised you let him. You will meet him again one day. He's an angel.*

...I would leave December 23rd open.

December 20, 1979

I STILL SMOKED.

In college, I played a character who smoked. By the time the play ended, I was in for two packs a day. Nothing had ever confused me as much as my relationship with smoking. I loved everything about smoking. And nothing I did disgusted me more. It had been five years now of trying to stop. I'd done almost everything. Several times I actually did it—stopped, cold turkey. For months. Then something would hit and I'd give myself permission to light up again. It was maddening. I did not understand myself. Why would I do something I hated, once finally freed from it? I couldn't understand how I could stop for several months and then start again because a friend on a boat offered me a cigarette.

One evening the month before, I was sitting in my living room late at night—miserable and angry I still hadn't quit. I stared at the last cigarette from my carton's last pack of Marlboros. I yelled out this promise to myself: "This, right here, right now, is the last cigarette I will ever smoke! I'm not playing a game this time. This is for real. This is my last smoke! Goodbye, my old friend."

I flipped her into the air and caught her deftly between my first and second finger—an impressive skill I'd learned over the last sixty thousand cigarettes. I caressed her gently like you would a lover you're about to leave. I was trying to savor every moment of this—from the strike of the match to the crackling sound of tobacco meeting flame. I deftly formed thick, nearly perfect smoke rings and then watched them float across the room, gently losing their integrity. I replayed all the moments I'd done this dance—in my Volkswagen, in motel rooms, after great meals, in a sleeping bag next to a girlfriend, waking up on the beach. I slowly savored her down to the nub. Then, benevolently, I laid her down and let her burn out on her own. A kind gesture of appreciation. And then… I was done. A new day was dawning.

For good measure, I scrunched up all the cigarette stubs in the ashtray and poured beer over them. It smelled lousy, but it convinced me this time I actually meant it.

I crawled into bed as a free man.

The next morning I awoke as a crazed man.

I was freaking desperate for a smoke! I completely brushed aside my promise from the evening before, like lint off a coat.

The internal conversation went like this: *I know I made a promise, but I didn't know I was going to feel like this! I can't live like this. Nobody can live like this! People on death row at least have smokes! I need to get into a better state of mind! I'll try it again, once I'm back in a stable relationship. I mean it. But right now I gotta have a smoke!*

I couldn't find any. I remembered last night's final cigarette was from my last pack. I panicked, now scrambling around looking under furniture, inside coat pockets. It was a two-minute drive to a convenience store, but I wouldn't make it. I needed a smoke—now!

Then, I looked over at the ashtray. Without even a thought, I rushed over and started straightening out the crumpled cigarette butts of last night. I think they're actually dried enough to light! Hunched over the ashtray in my underwear, I lit up the stubs of beer-flavored cigarettes. I took a deep, long, shaking pull, and once again, degraded myself to myself. Damn!

But that day, I tried another tactic; I asked a God I did not know to help me.

I have no business asking You anything. I don't talk to You. I don't bother You with requests or prayers. I'm not even certain You exist. But I hate that I smoke. It fills me with a self-loathing I don't even know how to describe. Look, so here's the deal. What if I don't smoke and You make it happen? That's right. I'm telling You I will not pick up a cigarette, but You've got to make it happen. I don't know if You entertain such requests, but I'm desperate here. If You parted the Red Sea, I imagine You can, if You want, keep me from picking up my next cigarette. So there it is. I know. Pitiful. I'm all screwed up. I don't even know if You bother to hear people like me. But starting right now, that's the deal. Okay?

I knew people quit smoking on their own, all the time. But this was me, and I couldn't.

Who did I think I was, throwing out this presumptuous challenge to God? But He chose to honor my request. I haven't smoked a cigarette since.

. . . Awakening . . .

Willpower can never defeat or resolve
the sins that entangle me.

. . . .

December 23, 1979

I LACED UP my New Balance 620s. I'd recently started running. I had stopped smoking three days before.

Suddenly, conversation with God started with one inaudible, but loudly perceived word:

Now.

It was my impetus to move forward. I had no idea into what. I only knew it was time to tell God what I now believed.

In the previous few weeks, I'd thought about where it would happen—the moment I'd tell Him I'm all in. Should I go into a church? Maybe I'd go up Camelback Mountain and shout it into the night air. Now the moment had come and I was sitting on a thrift store mattress in this dingy, bare, lonely guesthouse, which flooded every time it rained. It was the perfect place to represent the end of things. The end of my running from Him, the end of self-protection, of self-destruction, the end of fear, of pretending to be the victim of what I had mostly caused.

. . . Awakening . . .

I am never more authentically real than that moment I ask God in. It must overwhelm Him to have His love finally received.

, , , , , , , , , ,

God, it's John. I am so sorry. It's taken me so long. You've had to watch me go into so many strange and sad places. I want to do this right. I want it to take. Today, finally, no part of me is holding out. I have no other game plan. I am destroyed if You will not have me.

I want you to be my God. I believe You stayed on that cross for me, John Lynch. Somehow what You did was enough to make me clean if I believe it.

Today, I believe it.

Forgive me now, Jesus, for everything. It feels so wrong to ask You this. But You say that's what You want me to ask. I believe You were put on a cross and You allowed it, for me. You died for all my sedition; all my selfishness, all my rebellion and sickness… Yes, I finally now believe

You were raised from the dead.

I don't know what else to say...

Except this. Why would You do this for me? Why would You let me care? Why would You accept me after all I have done against You?

I don't want to become someone fake or pretend. But I'll do anything, go anywhere You want me. All I know is I want You, Jesus Christ. Wherever You are, You're the one I want. No one else. I'm calling this out loud for everyone in the universe to hear. This is John Lynch.

It probably wasn't as eloquent or well thought through. It was probably only a few sentences. But that's the best I can remember it.

John, that's pretty much how I remember it also.

December, 1979

FOR WEEKS, I could barely catch my breath—as though I could feel the synapses being rewired throughout my very being. Every moment felt supernatural and filled with endless, spiritual meaning. I was electric, pulsing with the experience of new life. I felt like I could walk up to someone in a department store and say, "You, sir, fall down on your knees and trust Jesus!"...and he would.

Over Christmas vacation that year, I devoured the Bible, nearly every waking hour. I wish there were some way to go back and experience all of it again. But I can't. No one can step into the same river twice. No one can feel brand new again. No one can repeat the first moment of worship. No one can enter from death into new life but once.

I know it doesn't happen that way for everyone. I wonder if God knew I needed a jolt to show me He was greater, more powerful than the drugs I'd taken, to overwhelm me. What God was doing for those days turned into weeks, made acid trips seem watered down.

I was so innocently looking for Him in every moment, every verse, every promise. I read the section in Matthew about the rich, young ruler. Jesus tested his sincerity by asking him to give up all his possessions to those in need.

So I did it.

I gave away my car to one of my students. I got rid of all my possessions except for a few clothes, books, cooking utensils, and several other basics. I sent checks to anyone I could remember borrowing money from. I nearly returned a dictionary and some masking tape I'd packed from my classroom when I left teaching.

I was naive. For sure, I was immature. I was probably butchering Scripture and yanking it into whatever I wanted it to say. But there was something so incredibly liberating about not yet knowing better. To run to obey God, not because I feared I would get in trouble, or because I was trying to assuage something, but because I would not miss any part of receiving God's love in full, wide-open obedience. That was no mistake.

John, it was in those moments you knew you had believed. You were done holding onto anything. You weren't trying to prove anything to Me. You only wanted everything with Me. You didn't want to miss a thing. Yes, you were, say, a bit loose with the Scriptures. But I'm not complaining.

On My Worst Day

1980

SO, WHAT HAPPENED? I wish I could isolate the moment. All I know is this: nobody did it to me. I pulled the bait and switch.

I think I presumed every day would be that intense, that jaw-dropping. I imagined I was one of the last humans to be rescued and now the end would come. The boat door was about to close. All I wanted to do was ride across the country on a ten-speed, with a sleeping bag and a daypack, to coffee shops, telling everyone to get on board, because the show was about to end. John Lynch had become a Christian! But weeks passed and I was still here. Slowly, I realized I could still be sad, and I was not impervious to people cutting me off in traffic. I discovered my reactions and wrong affections had not been healed. I was experiencing stupidly immoral thoughts.

I would tell Jesus, "Don't listen to that thought. Please, I didn't mean it." Then my thinking moved to this: *Of course! I knew I'd screw this up. God goes to all the work of bringing me to Him and now I've got Him disappointed. I do this to everyone. They all eventually leave. It's who I am. Damn!*

...See, now I'm swearing!

But I knew I could not live without what I had found. I would not lose it. In that moment, like smoke under a door, it crept back in. Shame.

. . . Awakening . . .

Increased devotion and diligence will not make me feel close to God again. Believing His never-changing affection will renew my joy.

. . . .

I guess I thought to get back feeling close to God it would take the same methods which once gave me applause and success: increased willpower, diligence, ought, berating myself to care more. That lie would spread its tentacles through my soul for many, many years.

It took so little time from first trusting Him to arrive here: **The second part of my life I spent trying to make myself worthy of the love I had found.**

I guess I could have challenged the lie: *Hey, wait. Hold on. I didn't earn this love from God. I didn't figure this thing out. I didn't do anything heroic to get it. It was entirely one way. He invaded my destruction. Nothing I'm experiencing suggests He's one to bless me with happiness or withhold it by the constancy of my devotion. He knows me. He knew I was smoking three packs a day, dropping cheap acid, and lying on my resumé that I'd done standup comedy in L.A.*

I wonder what would have happened if I'd simply called out to God: *Hey, I'm scared. I don't know what to do. I feel like I'm messing things up. I've spent the entire last week hiding from You, trying to figure out some formula to make it right—to make You happy with me again. I don't even know what I'm doing. I'm confused... And maybe disappointed. Is it all right to tell You that? I wanted it to always be like those first few weeks. Anyway, I'm freaked out and feeling this old familiar sense—like someone is about to leave me again. Don't go away from me. I've waited for You all my life. Please. I have nowhere else to go now.*

If I can know You're there, that You're not angry or disgusted and this is the way it's going to be, I'm totally good. I just need to know I haven't screwed this whole thing up. I'd like a sign or something right now. But I have the idea You probably don't often do magic when You're trying to form faith. That sounded like I know what I'm talking about. I don't. It's something I heard someone say. Then I repeat it and make it sound like me. I do that. I make crap up. Anyway, I love You so much. I can't make it go away if I wanted to. Help.

Love, John.

But I didn't do that.

My fear of losing this ecstatic experience of Him drowned out such logic. I almost didn't care whether He operated out of peevish, manipulative jealousy or not. I wanted the feeling back.

When compelled, I don't know many humans more self-restrictively disciplined towards a goal than me. So I reared back and spent my best effort trying to find a way to get God to be pleased with me.

. . . Awakening . . .

*Nothing deadens us more than learning to
perform from duty and ought, what we once*

did as the natural response of a new heart.

. . . .

And my joy walked back into the shadows.

I didn't talk to anyone about it. Nobody told me they were doing a similar thing. But I soon found it was an unspoken way of life in most faith communities. No matter how much we sang of His unconditional love and sovereign power, we trusted more in our ability to keep ourselves in good stead. We were becoming religiously self-righteous and increasingly miserable.

1981

AFTER SEVERAL MONTHS, it became increasingly apparent Jesus was not going to time His return to my new faith. A friend, who'd been watching me devour the Bible, told me, "There's this place where people talk about God and the Scriptures all day long, every day."

"You're kidding me! Where is this place?"

"They call it seminary."

"I must go to this seminary place you speak of."

So I left my teaching job and headed to Talbot seminary in California, driving another VW Bug. My boss had given it to me. I had spent a thousand of my three-thousand-dollar teaching retirement to get it running. I poured a quart of oil into her almost twice a week.

I left Arizona with enough money to cover part of a semester of classes. How did I think I was going to pay for four years of full-time classes in a Masters program for which I had zero background? I guess I hadn't yet experienced a time yet where God had not met my needs the way I thought He should. I thought it was part of this new supernatural life. If I'm attempting something that's right, why wouldn't He absolutely provide?

Arriving at seminary, I was a longhaired hippie with very little understanding of any Christian language or culture. I spent the first few nights in the parking lot studying my Hebrew declensions with a flashlight in my car. Learning a new language, especially one that reads backward, was overwhelming and other-worldly after a decade of aggressively burning brain cells.

It didn't take me long to find a part-time job at a private Christian after-school program. It paid me enough to afford a dumpy shared apartment, where Campus Crusade wrestlers routinely left lasagna-covered frying pans in the shower. I fished a mattress out of the apartment's storage. It had a large hole in one corner. Cockroaches were emerging from it. This was definitely a low point in my housing timeline.

After several weeks, the owner of the school took me to lunch.

"John, we're so pleased with the work you're doing at our school. Would you consider coming on as a full-time teacher?"

"I'm honored, but I don't think I should. I came out here to go to seminary. I left my world back in Phoenix. I'm convinced God wants me in seminary. I know me. If I start working full time I'd never get through seminary. I left teaching to do something with God's Word. It doesn't feel right to have moved out here to do what I already left. I'm so sorry. It's a kind and generous offer."

I lived with the faith, and probably some presumption, God would get the money figured out somehow. I think God kindly chose to cover the absurdly grandiose checks I was writing.

A week later, the owner of the school took me to lunch again. "So, how are you paying for your seminary degree?"

"I'm using money left from my teaching retirement."

"How much?"

"All of it. Enough to pay for this first quarter."

"How are you paying for next quarter? It comes up in about two weeks, doesn't it?"

"Yes, it does. I don't quite yet know what will happen. I guess I'm trusting God will take care of me."

He got quiet for a while, soaking his fries in the au jus from his French dip sandwich. "Well, I also think God has you here to be in seminary. If you'd let us, my wife and I would like to pay for your entire time in seminary. Your books, insurance, and all of your tuition. I'd only hope you'd consider working in the afternoon program as long as your studies allow you to."

I remember being incredibly grateful and excited beyond words that God had revealed how I was going to do seminary. But I was not astonished.

…This section was not supposed to spill out this way. Writing it is convicting me of a way of life I once knew and now teach about knowing.

Trust.

It wasn't presumption. I'd sensed real conviction from a real, actively communicating God that I should go to seminary. He knew all along how He was going to do it. I was convinced He knew. I can't remember the last time I knew with such conviction.

I'm sorry. I want to present a steady, gradually maturing man, released by the truths of grace. The truth is I often believed better back then than I do now. I can live now in much clutching fear of the future. I can think about positioning and covering bases more than trusting. I'm not quite sure what to do with this. It doesn't fit a clean narrative arch. It doesn't build a compelling argument. If I'm truthful, much of my life conflicts with what I know to be true.

John, you are not nearly as confident that I'll come through as you were back then. In fairness, I have done many things, allowed many things, did not stop many things you thought I should, would, must. It has rocked your world. It is hard for Me to watch you scuff at the pavement, trying to figure Me out, trying to reconcile My goodness with your pain and broken expectations.

I cannot let you write and speak continually about Me without your authenticity being tested. Otherwise, your words will degenerate into untested and powerless slogans.

What you are teaching is largely true. But you do not always live it or believe it magnificently. Humans don't mature in a straight line. You and I are in a love relationship. These days, you've been hurt, confused, and devastated at what I would allow into your world. You are grieving. I know you do not always trust Me. I am not angry or disappointed with you when you doubt My ways. I am only proud you would admit it here. If you want validation your life is working splendidly, you'll find it in your admission two paragraphs back. You're not nearly as good a liar as you once were...

1982

I WAS NOW living with two married couples in Santa Fe Springs. They were friends from my church back in Phoenix.

One spring evening, for the first time, I saw it. Who I risked becoming—a higher-educated, striving, religious Pharisee. I saw the life I was forming, living out the implications of trying to please God by enough fervent effort and self-denial.

I was in my bedroom, trying to pray. They were in the living room watching an inane television show. It was turned up too loud. Sitcom television sounds even more garish from another room.

My friends sounded like drunks in a roomful of drunks. They were wheezing in laughter. I would one day wish I could be back with them in that moment, wheezing along with them. But at the time I was trying so hard to prove I was cut from different cloth. That I was more sold out, more passionate, more faithful, more attentive to God. Godly people do not fritter their time away in noisy and cheap laughter. Only later would I discover I was only attempting to disprove what my shame wanted to convince me of—that I was not enough. I was tied up tight in chains of performance. I was judging my friends in the other room as halfhearted Laodiceans, not caring enough to be fully used by God.

Whatever I did over the next hour was anything but prayer. I was filled with seething, arrogant religiosity. God was out watching television, laughing with my friends.

At some point, I whispered out in a muffled scream: "I don't get You. I'm trying so hard to do things right and You don't show up! Those people are out there not caring about the things of God and they're having a great time. Listen to them! Me, I'm miserable. I hate this. I'm watching the clock, every minute, trying to put in an hour, like those famous saints who said if they didn't get in two hours of prayer, the day was wasted." Many of us face a time where we are tempted to blame God for not doing enough in us, fast enough, impressively enough. We become weary from doing all the things to impress Him, expecting more return. "I'm trying, God. I'm trying! Help me. Tell me what You want me to do. I want to be a godly man. I want to do great things. I want to get over the garbage in me. Why don't You make it happen? I'm doing everything I know how to do."

This was actually a very good moment; when pride could turn into humility.

John, I wish you could walk out there and be with your friends. At this moment, they are throwing cornbread at each other and watching reruns of Mannix. I was out there with them, moments ago. So, this is an important moment. You are growing weary of trying to figure out how to please Me. You've been trying so hard for so long. There is endless difference between straining for My favor by doing enough right and allowing My Spirit to draw out the good you now actually want to do. You are using your same old willpower and discipline to behave how you think I would want. Tonight you are witnessing the sham of your own performing. You're less than three years into your faith and completely miserable. I never wanted that for you. Have you forgotten how astonishing those first few months were? You were free, alive, and we talked like lifelong friends. Then you got religious on Me.

So, you had to wear yourself out. Now you're becoming open to a new living out this faith in Me. This is where it will start to get fun.

. . . Awakening . . .

Many try so hard to become godly instead of trusting they already are.

, , , ...

On My Worst Day

1983

"I'VE HEARD ALL about you. It just seems like a guy like you and girl like me should go out."

She was flirting with me! No one had flirted with me in a long, long time. I was in Phoenix for a friend's wedding. And this unguarded, funny, attractive woman was playing me like a cheap banjo!

Stacey Marie Pilger.

I'd seen her before. I'd stared at her during services at Open Door Fellowship, where my high school students brought me when I first risked to enter a church. She was captivating. She was beautiful. She still is.

I thought she'd have little memory of that evening. I was only a guy she didn't know. What did she have to lose? She was so full of spontaneous, unrehearsed, unfettered fun. I left her presence undone. Whatever smitten is, I was it—stumbling to my car like a smiling, drunken man.

The next day, I was at a reception for close friends and relatives of the bride and groom. I was in the backyard talking to the groom's grandmother. Not out of kindness, but because she was not getting up anytime soon. She was a safe place for me to hide out among strangers.

Stacey walked into the backyard and noticed me.

God quickly went to work on my behalf. God directly spoke words to her.

That man, right there. He is going to be your husband. Go talk to him.

All afternoon, we flitted around each other, like geeky junior high kids at a school dance.

The next morning in church, she noticed me staring at her. She composed a note and slipped it into my shirt pocket after the service. It started with these words: "Blue-eyed one, I've noticed you..." The wonderful, soaring note ended with her phone number. I found a mirror to see if I have blue eyes.

I was toast. Toast.

Stacey says God gave me to her to open up a life of significance, of grace—with children raised in tenderness, experiencing the immediacy of Jesus.

God gave me Stacey as my object lesson of my newfound theology of grace. All other women before her loved me if or because of. Two decades of women told me they loved me. I think they did. Until they saw how messed up I was. My weaknesses, my fear, my irrational outbursts of panic eventually caused them to leave. When I was no longer the life of the party, they left the party.

Stacey was the first to love me just because. When I was not on my game, when my breath was bad, in my pajamas with oily hair. When she saw the obsessiveness, insecurity, and jealousy in me. She was the first woman to convince me that who I am when I am not "on" was more than enough. Her love has shaped me more than any other person's on this planet.

I get lost in lies that can still keep me from the truth of who Christ is in me. I can write and speak about the truths I love so much better than I can live them. So God gave me a woman who refuses to believe the lies I tell myself, whose playfulness draws me out from my head.

I always feared something horrible would happen to our world—that Stacey would go south, drift away in bitterness. In truth, when things do go south for us, it's Stacey who holds us together.

I wrote this into my phone, on the patio of a restaurant at Crystal Cove, at our twenty-eighth anniversary dinner: *Today, twenty-eight years ago, we both took this high-stakes gamble that the other would stay in the arena. That day, she couldn't be sure, she didn't know if I would revert back to my old life, my checking out into isolation, medicating, and running to the next place. She didn't know if I'd continue to allow Jesus in, to be everything for me, for us, and whatever family He would give us. I didn't know if she would be courageous, if she would stay in the hard times, if she would be faithful to me, if she would keep trusting Him when it seems like He's forgotten about her. You don't know what the other will do. You think you know. You fall in love and hope.*

But we put so much on the line, in those vows—trusting God to protect us, trusting the other to show up each day, even after we've failed or been adrift for so long. I don't know why we're still here, deeply in love with each other, in a deeply hard period. Why us? Many don't make it. They are not less good, less loving, or less trusting of God. I only know He is good and has been good to us. Beyond that, I'm not sure I can explain anything. But I do know this: after having seen the very worst life can throw at us, I'd choose her over every single woman in history... save for Ruth from the Old Testament. I've said it before; I would have dumped Stacey early on for that woman. Stacey would have pushed me off a pier for a chance to marry the patriarch Joseph.

But having missed out on those two, we've done all right settling for each other. I'm in for twenty-eight more. Then I'm out of here. Mark it.

June 3
1985

THE SUNDAY BEFORE our wedding, I was invited to speak at Open Door Fellowship. It was overwhelming to speak to the community who took me in during the first year of my faith. I prepared a message out of chapter three of Zechariah—my exegetical passage for my second-year Hebrew class. The passage presents a vision of the pre-incarnate Jesus defending Joshua, the post-exilic leader of Israel. The evil one was the accusing prosecuting attorney. God the Father was the judge in the case. It's one of those wild and woolly Old Testament sections convincing me God must like rock and roll. There are forty ways to tell this truth, but God went creative and acted some of the stuff out, with others, in a dream sequence!

If there is a supremely important passage of grace in the Old Testament, this is it. Satan was accusing Israel of failing to be a defensible witness to God. "Joshua was clothed with filthy garments and standing before the angel" Zechariah 3:3 NASB. Satan knew if he could discredit him, the entire line of the Messiah would unravel. In the middle of the accusations, "the angel of the Lord" spoke. Whenever the article "the" (rather than "an") is in front of "angel of the Lord" in the Old Testament, most scholars agree we are watching a pre-incarnate appearance of Jesus. Wow! He rebuked Satan, then turned to Joshua and in one sentence handed out the freedom from guilt He would one day purchase. "Remove the filthy garments from him… See, I have taken your iniquity away from you and will clothe you with festal robes" Zechariah 3:4 NASB.

I'm not sure I will ever spend forty minutes doing more of what I was put on this earth to do. I was frenetically working my way around the stage as if in that vision's very courtroom. Absolutely locked in the moment, I was having so much fun, I didn't want it to end. I didn't want to top out on one of my first messages when I had several thousand left to go! But I think that's the case.

Stacey and I were in Lake Tahoe on our honeymoon when we got word that Bill Thrall, the pastor who started Open Door, said these words the following Sunday: "That was the finest message ever preached in this church."

The man who spoke those words had been the primary preacher in this church. In that instant, I knew I was a preacher.

At 3:45 a.m., twenty-eight years later, several thousand messages into this craft, I would write these words about what I have stumbled into: *Early Sunday morning is the most surreal four hours for some who preach. You get up in the middle of the night because you alone know the sum total of your study during the week has given you pages of sincerely good notes, clever turns of phrase, and skilled segues, but no real message from God to man. So once again you panic and begin to beg God to show up. The ideas which sounded clever and insightful days before now barely hold even your interest. You ask God to give you something at the last second which would give something to someone. Life. Something to convince you that you're not bluffing this morning.*

And then it happens. New thoughts, channels of entry, my heart engaged, courage to type dangerous, unrehearsed thoughts, vulnera-

bility, and… slowly something like the very heart of God. That entire mechanically correct but hollow message I was willing, last evening, to foist upon a congregation, transforms in front of my very eyes. I've lost interest in whether it's clever or eloquent. For the first time all week, I'm believing what I will now preach. For twenty-eight years I've woken up before bakers and newspaper carriers, gambling God would do this. I wish He'd do it on Wednesday or Thursday, but He doesn't. And now, sitting in the dark with a cup of coffee, He did it again. No one may even notice the difference. But I will. It has kept me from feeling like paid clergy these last twenty-eight years. So, now I'm off to perform this high-wire act. I'm asking Him to turn this message into what He'd like for the one who risks walking over from the cheap apartments across the street, fearing God no longer hears her or wants to live through her… How did I get this privilege?

July, 1985

WE RETURNED TO Los Angeles, married. I excitedly handed a tape of my Zechariah message to the pastor of the church I'd been attending during seminary. I wanted him to be proud of me. He listened to it and passed it on to the head of the district in the denomination I expected to candidate for as I prepared to graduate. Several weeks later, the pastor called me to meet for breakfast. A venerable and soft-spoken, white-haired man, he was deeply beloved and respected within the denomination. He'd been in this role for decades.

Have you ever had that experience where everything in front of you suddenly morphs into a slow-motion crash, with the sound of screeching metal giving way to explosions?

His response to my message shocked my very being. The wreck was formed of these words:

"John, I listened to your message. What I heard was immature, self-seeking, and self-serving. It was too dramatic and emotional. I tried to finish it, but couldn't. My recommendation is you not go into the ministry for quite a while. Take some time to grow up, maybe volunteering with the youth at this church after you graduate. Preaching is a very serious and sacred endeavor. You did not treat it with the gravity it demands. That message was unacceptable. It offended me on many levels. Here's your tape back."

I have no idea what happened next.

I vaguely remember crying the entire way up the I-605 from Long Beach to Whittier.

I don't think I've ever since worked on a message as hard as I had on that one. I truly believed it was the best I could ever hope to do, with a message allowing me to be the most fully John Lynch, representing God's heart.

All my life, I'd doubted my own sincerity. Only these last several years in Christ was I beginning to believe I could trust my authenticity was growing. Now here was a venerable religious authority questioning not only my capacity but also my character and motives. Everything was on the line at that moment. I would either allow someone to protect me or I would secretly bluff and pretend I believed my identity in Christ when I no longer did.

It was so hard to tell Stacey. I feared even she'd change her perception of me. I feared the same when I called Bill. I was frozen. I didn't know how to move forward. "If I am wrong about that which I felt singularly most proud of and convinced of, then what do I know about myself?"

Bill listened patiently to the entire story over the phone. After a silence, he said, "Well, I'm no prophet, but it appears this man did not enjoy the message or your presentation of it." He started laughing. I laughed too.

"John, maybe you do need to mature. Maybe a lot. But no one should take the permission to critique and rebuke another unless they're willing to draw in closer to the solution. If you want, when you graduate, you could come to Open Door. I would commit to work with you on the issues of your maturing as much as you would like."

I'd been already candidating for church staff roles. One church in Oxnard had offered me a position as a "Christian Education Curriculum Director." One should probably not accept a job with a title whose meaning one does not understand.

"Look, John, this man's critique has forced you to form a conclusion about who you are. There are many people who can do a number of things well. You are not one of them. But many have spoken to me about the message you preached here. I have not many times experienced the presence of God in the Word like I did that day. You're a preacher, John. You may be young in the faith and immature in your experience, but if you can be convinced to stop speaking, many in the future will lose out. I can't think of a worse thing for you to do than to find a Christian job so you can have a religious title. Give me the phone number of those people who want you to be their curriculum director. They're making a horrible mistake. You'd be terrible at it. John, I'd be honored to help you get started speaking at camps, retreats, and conferences. You could speak at our midweek service, to get some experience."

"You'd do that?"

"To keep those poor folks from having you as their curriculum director, I'd do a lot."

On that day, I experienced protection. Without it, I imagine walking around crippled, wounded, and self-doubting; one of the best theologically trained shoe repairmen in town. Without his commitment to me, to stand with me in the middle of my fear, insecurity, and immaturity, I wouldn't have made it. I wonder how many thousands of hopeful young God-lovers have been sideswiped, without a Bill Thrall to brace them.

Two years later, in his backyard: "So, I think it's time for you to take the pulpit. I'll stay and help develop leaders. You're the one who should be leading us in the pulpit."

Something amazing happens when we stumble into spiritual safety. Many of us have never known it. We aren't even sure it exists. We've existed in the realm of "following Jesus" in a culture of being more right, accurate, and exact about our theological positions. We can go from theological conviction to creed to manifesto. But we're still on our guard.

. . . Awakening . . .

We can hold the most orthodox positions with exacting accuracy and still be a lousy parent, unwise boss, or a board member no one wants to be near.

, , , , , , , , , , ,

All the while, we convince ourselves we've put our ladder up against the right wall. But at night, it may occur to us... *I don't know how to let my guard down. And I have a suspicion I make others all around me feel less safe.*

. . . Awakening . . .

Safety allows me to ask questions I can't when I'm proving myself. It allows me to trust another to describe me to me.

. . . .

1985

. . . Awakening . . .

*The only one I cannot protect is myself. I
must trust the commitment of another.*

. . . .

THESE ARE DEEPLY important words. But they remain largely
untouched until someone comes along who chooses, for your benefit,
to earn your trust and offer his or her commitment. Then you have
a real chance to take the wild-eyed gamble to no longer self-protect.

I place this story here, in 1985, only because this is when my relationship with Bill Thrall began. I still don't know why Bill took an
interest in me. But if I could get a friend like Bill then there must be
others out there for everyone else. This particular story has a dispro-
portionate number of "Awakenings." That's because much of the
wisdom I carry has been instilled in me through God using a particular individual to teach me. None of these "Awakenings" belong to
me. They were formed in a community I found myself privileged to
stumble into after seminary—Open Door Fellowship. But they were
largely taught to me by the commitment, modeling, and intention-
ality of my big brother in the faith.

Bill is one of my very best friends. He has believed in me. He knows almost all of my issues, faults, and flaws. But he also sees the real me beyond them. He trusts God's love and grace. He will not allow me to wallow in my failures, even when they have affected him directly. I honestly think he would value my influence and success as much, if not more, than his own. Who does that? I guess those who have trusted Jesus with themselves. This is the goal of the instruction from the writers of the New Testament. To work hard to earn permission in, to love; always earning trust so that when we want to give ourselves permission to fail, there would be someone we'd trust to bring us in from the cold.

. . . Awakening . . .

Trying to fix me won't help. But if I don't have to hide, my life issues will begin to be resolved.

. . . .

Who do you know who knows you so well and so beautifully that you don't have to hide anything? For years, Bill taught me these words: "What if there was a place so safe that the worst of me could be known and I would discover that I was loved more, not less, in the telling of it?" Remember my story about the abuse at the boxcars? It was Bill that I first told. His commitment to me, along with Stacey's, allowed me to no longer hide. The result has been that my unresolved issues continue to have a chance to vitally heal. Bill also taught me that it is less important for things to ever get fixed, and more important that we no longer have to hide anything. Can you imagine the difference that reality creates in a family, in a marriage? What difference would that make in a church staff, where people have come, often from performance-driven faith cultures, carrying all manner of religiously super-charged hiddenness?

. . . *Awakening* . . .

The courage to tell on myself about the wrong I am intending to do is one of the most heroic actions I can take.

. . . .

To tell on ourselves before we act on the intention is a stunning display of the new life in us. We are choosing to no longer give ourselves permission to do something that moments ago we were willing to risk integrity and health to gain. Such a choice is revolutionarily supernatural. It also happens to be the only thing we can do to stop sin once it begins to present itself to our consciousness. No self-discipline, no intense striving, no promises, no beating ourselves up, nothing else will stop sin's power once it forms. Any means other than telling on ourselves is utterly pitiful. We are trying to resist a failure we've already given ourselves permission to do! The very act of resistance only heightens the anticipated pleasure of the acting out. But the moment I finally risk to tell another of the sin I am intending to do, everything changes. For that particular issue, in this particular cycle, the darkness loses its power. And I find myself safely home.

This is how it works. "For sin shall not be master over you, for you are not under law but under grace" Romans 6:14 NASB. Grace gives me, in my obsession and compulsions, a way home. It's glorious!

. . . Awakening . . .

The objective is not to build communities appearing to have sin under control. The objective is to nurture a place safe enough where people can stop faking they have sin under control.

. . . .

Such a community is messy but utterly healthy. Those who live in it become free and they end up sinning less. A leader who trusts this way of life is able to stand in the tension of such a community; even such a work environment. There will always be demand, structure, expectations, and something worth doing, all being done with great diligence. It's all a matter of how this good work gets done best. Many leaders never learn that the best environment for great accomplishment is an environment of trust, safety, and authenticity. Any other approach misses the quality of relationship that honors the reason we were doing the work in the first place.

. . . Awakening . . .

*If you gain permission into my life I will allow you to
stand with me and to challenge the lies I tell myself.*

. . . .

There are few more meaningful gifts than to be given such
permission. It is worth whatever cost it has taken to earn such trust.
It gives an invaluable gift to those you protect. It allows the self-entitlement they offer themselves to fail. The moment we stop pretending
a righteousness we didn't think we possessed, but later discovered we
actually do, it changes just about everything. We get to trust love
from God and others. This causes us to love more and sin less. And I
get to be honest about whatever has not yet changed. This has value
for more than us. Those outside the community of faith in Jesus lose
their reason for staying away. Our hypocrisy. Most know Jesus is real.
It's us, bluffing a façade that looks nothing like Jesus that freaks them
out. Once we can be authentic with what has not yet changed, they
can finally relate to us. And it diminishes none of Christ's power to
them. To watch us give up faking, bluffing, hiding, and hypocrisy is a
miracle few of them thought Jesus was even capable of.

Know this, so I don't pretend a maturity more than I carry.
Anything you read in this book that hints at transferable wisdom,
insight, or love—Bill's fingerprints are nearby. I love him so. I am
committed to him. I have protected him and will continue to protect
him in any way I am allowed for the rest of his days. After all, he
trusted God and took a risk on me. The guy who still had dope resin
on his fingertips.

1988

I STUMBLED INTO a community of grace while wildly theologically opposed to the concept. I didn't learn this way of life in seminary. These young believers at Open Door Fellowship probably didn't even know they were influencing me so strongly. They didn't even know how to cogently articulate what was happening to them! But I watched them live with each other so well. It all got through to me.

For two years I was preaching to them all I knew: a "man-up, buck-up" pile of theological-sounding self-importance and parroted platitudes. They endured it. I was boldly proclaiming a moralistic sin-management doctrine while hiding the pain of my own compromise and immaturity.

It happens all the time, almost everywhere. We have a gift and it finds us a platform. We fall in love with being important. People actually think we know what we're talking about. The greatest drive is to keep our platform because people start to admire us.

So we create a pretend, competent, assured self, hoping to buy ourselves some time. But it makes us less healthy and less teachable. They don't know we're lying. God still is growing them up in spite of our carefully polished mush. So a gifted, clever, funny, articulate young preacher blusters and poses as having a maturity and wisdom he does not actually possess.

Looking back, I can't understand why they didn't stop me. It's like they had a meeting. "Anyone else notice this kid is bluffing? Maybe if we stay close, eventually he'll catch on we're not buying his line. He may let us in. Then we get to watch the kid mature into these truths. Either way, he's still pretty funny."

So a community gradually teaches a preacher what to preach.

. . . Awakening . . .

It's exceedingly difficult for anyone to understand grace as anything other than a theological position unless they experience it in community.

. . . .

I remember the Sunday it happened. Some call it a "grace awakening." For months, I'd been studying Ephesians and been rocked by Paul's overwhelming account of what Christ has completed in us already. He teaches the only way to live is to trust who we are in Christ and who Christ is in us. He pleads we try no other method to face our sin and failures. I was arguing with Paul all week before preaching this passage, "...be renewed in the spirit of your mind and put on the new self, which in the likeness of God has been created in righteousness and holiness of the truth" Ephesians 4:23-24 NASB. I kept rereading Romans 7 and 8, Philippians 3:9, 2 Corinthians 5:21, and Galatians 2:20. They were forming a chorus convincing me I'm a saint who still has sin but is adored, rather than a saved sinner who is a grave disappointment to God. *Yeah, but what about personal responsibility? What about fighting the good fight? What about living with fear and trembling?* For so long those verses appeared to demand a buck-up response. Now they were slamming up against this new conviction of a Christ who had already radically changed me and was now maturing me in His perfect timing.

A friend had recently given me a copy of Brennan Manning's *The Ragamuffin Gospel*. Manning destroyed me with his ragged and brutal admission of his pretense, arrogance, and pretending. He built a case for trusting only in Christ's power in me and the unwillingness of God to receive even my own condemnation. He was exposing my charade.

That Sunday morning's message began with an apology: "Something is happening inside me. I've been bluffing to you, trying to impress you with my seminary insights and knowledge of the original languages. I actually don't know enough of either to understand what I'm talking about. I've talked tough and told you to be sold out to God. The truth is, I'm not doing this life very well. I'm in a continual battle of willpower against sin. I'm losing. Badly. I have no idea how to communicate what I am beginning to understand about living out of a new identity. It's still pretty elusive to me. I'm sorry it has taken me this long. I only know I am tired of forcing this Bible to say what I think it should say. I've wanted it to tell you off, so I could get you people to be better. It has been ugly and humbling to realize I'm the one who doesn't know how to be better. That's all I've got right now."

God set me on a course that morning to discover how to articulate this way of life in Christ. This time it would not be in isolation, but in a community learning it together.

Jesus had been waiting for me to start reading the Word without a shame and moralistic filter. Only then could I understand Him saying this to me:

> *You and I are absolutely and completely now fused with each other. Your strength, joy, hope, peace, everything will come from risking this to be true. We are melded as precious metals. Yes, I am God and you are human. But the unthinkable has happened. All of Me infused into all of you. It is impossible to discern where I begin and you end. I am no longer God up there with you down here. I am now closer than a burning bush, a vision, or even a disciple sitting next to Me. I am now identified by you, My dear friend.*
>
> *Your true identity is Christ in you. You may absolutely put your entire weight upon this. It most perfectly honors what the cross and the resurrection accomplished. Please don't shy from this in some religious sense of it being too good to be true or beyond your worth. This declares your worth. Enjoy this with all your being. Don't waste a day pretending it is not true. I promise you it is.*

. . . Awakening . . .

We're all screwed up. Only bad religion can cause us to pretend we're not. We're still compromised and maturing, even on our best day. It's just better to know we are.

. . . .

1989

GOD WAS NOW starting to give me stories, pictures, scenes, pieces to act out, ways to release this grace that had captured me. I want to share a piece that I wrote for an event I spoke at in West Covina, California. It was one of the first times someone asked me for a copy of something I had written. This is still one of the most important ways God has given me to see this glorious way of life that Jesus offers to us. I want you to have it:

If I know I have worth because of His choice of fully loving me, then I don't have to manufacture a reason to be loved. I can, instead, love you and offer you affirmation and attention.

If I know His acceptance of me is irrevocable, then I don't have to gossip about you and tear you down in order to build myself up. I can instead, protect your heart and build you up.

If I know I'm loved by Him only because of His good pleasure, then I don't have to compete with you in parenting, finances, godliness, home decorating, accolades, or friends. I can, instead, work for your success and see your success as mine also.

If I know I'm rich in Him already in everything that matters, then I don't have to prove my wealth in finances, status, looks, career, competence, notoriety, or talent. I can, instead, use my time to pay attention to your needs.

If I know that I'll be taken care of by God's sovereign protection, then I don't have to preoccupy myself—scheming and pressuring myself to get ahead and do things to get noticed. I can, instead, look around and see who's hurting.

If I know that God is already pleased with me in Christ, then I don't have to busy myself with proving my worth. I can rest, relax, play, and give my full attention to my family, and at the end of the day, smile and sleep well.

If I know that God's gifts of biggest and best don't always go to those who please Him most, then I don't have to make "success" my driving passion. I can, instead, let character, integrity, faithfulness, and love be my drive.

If I know God is in control of my moment-to-moment needs, then I don't have to control others. I can, instead, free them through my trust in them.

If I know God isn't judging me by a standard of who is the best leader, or who has the most authority, then I don't have to worry about positioning myself. I can, instead, submit to your strengths and protect your weaknesses.

If I know God is for me, then I don't have to prove myself by my righteousness. I can listen to you and let your heart teach mine.

If I know there is no dream out there that God will deny me because of lack of self-attentiveness, then I don't have to regret where I am in life right now. I can then be used by God to foster His dreams for you.

If I know God is always gracious toward me, then I don't have to be gruff, demanding, intolerant, or judging of you. I can then offer grace, mercy, forgiveness, and acceptance to you.

If I know that I am a new creature, crucified with Christ, indwelt by the Holy Spirit, forgiven completely, justified, redeemed, and sanctified, with Jesus and His intimate love present every single moment, then I no longer have to beat myself up, mistrust myself, pretend I can't please God, or pretend I can't live for Him. I can then start to experience and enjoy my sweet Savior every single day of my life.

On My Worst Day

1990

I ALMOST PEED my pants, right in front of my audience.

I was in the middle of an illustration on a Sunday morning. All of us started laughing and couldn't stop. It was one of those times where you think you'll stop laughing, and then somebody in the audience snorts and you're all back on the train.

At one point, I stood there and stared out upon this congregation with tears of laughter in my eyes. I was struggling to catch my breath.

It was like we were speaking words behind our laughter to each other:

Audience: "John, we never thought we'd get to be like this in a church. It's incredibly exhilarating. But do you think God likes that we're playing around right now? This story you're telling—it has no point, no value. It's like a lead guitar solo in a spiritual song. We want to believe our God values all of this. But it does seem sort of wrong."

Me: "I hope He's delighted. I'm banking everything on the fact that He's in it all. That He enjoys it all. That it's all part of this incredible being He's remade each of us to be. If we're in Him, it's all God stuff. This enjoyment, it too is created by Him! I have a feeling He's laughing as hard as we are."

Audience: "We were hoping you'd say that."

. . . Awakening . . .

*God is not afraid to risk the consequences
of what we do with His grace.*

. , . . , ... , . .

I could have landed in ten thousand other communities, where there would have been a built-in religious expectation I would've had to fake my way through. To be in a place that was risking to trust I am Christ in me felt so freeing and dangerous all at the same time. We trusted we had new hearts that could be trusted. We trusted God with the pace of each other's maturity, humor, and kindness. And many of us were getting healed in the gamble...

. . . Awakening . . .

*One of the most freeing moments in my life is to
discover that who I am as a Christian and who
I really am have become the same person.*

. , . . , ... , .

1990

BACK IN 1983, Mike McDevitt and I were watching a rerun of the '60s television show *Bonanza* while we ate lunch in the home I shared with the McDevitts and several others.

Long story short: "Little Joe" Cartwright was the handsome son of Ben Cartwright. Ben was the wise, kind, and benevolent patriarch of this wealthy ranching family. This particular episode ended with the two of them working through a breakup with a young woman Little Joe had been seeing. Little Joe was sad.

Ben was about to make a final, concluding, profound statement. It's what he did. He was a strong man of few words, but the ones he chose carried immense weight and should be heeded by his children. He put his hand on Little Joe's shoulder and said these words, which apparently would make sense of all the heartache Little Joe was facing. It was the last moment before the episode ended and the theme music started up.

What both Mike and I heard was this exact phrase: "Bubbleen, Little Joe. Bubbleen."

I looked over at Mike. "Uh…Did he just say…?"

Mike answered, "Bubbleen. He said, 'Bubbleen, Little Joe. Bubbleen.'"

Me: "That's what I heard! He can't have said 'Bubbleen'! It means nothing."

Mike: "I think his exact words were 'Bubbleen, Little Joe.

Bubbleen.'"

There was no rewinding in those days. Unless you worked as a film editor at the network station, one shot was all the consumer got.

We must have laughed for twenty minutes about "Bubbleen." There's no other phrase it could have been! We substituted dozens of alternatives, trying to give them the benefit of the doubt. But nothing worked. What important phrase of help from Ben to Little Joe could possibly rhyme with "Bubbleen"?

"Break my spleen, Little Joe. Break my spleen."

"My real name is Lorne Greene, Little Joe. Lorne Greene."

"Bub, we're on the big screen, Little Joe. On the big screen."

"Boy, you're lean, Little Joe. Boy, you're lean."

"Let's get out of this scene, Little Joe. Let's get out of this scene." Nothing fit it.

Six months after that, I moved and didn't see Mike much at all for nine years. But I told the "Bubbleen" story dozens and dozens of times to friends, wherever I went. I've shared it when I taught at conferences and camps. I've used it as an illustration in a Sunday morning message. Maybe I've been hoping someone can shed some light on it and put this mystery to bed.

My relatively new friend, Bob Ryan, had heard me tell this story in different settings many times already. He was a freelance graphic designer and was teaming with a local design artist on a magazine project.

Bob called me. "John, I'm working with a guy named Mike McDevitt. Could this be the Mike McDevitt from the 'Bubbleen' story? He's a design artist in town."

"Wow! I didn't know Mike was in town. Yes, that's probably him!" Bob said only this, before he hung up: "I've got an idea."

Four days later. Bob met with Mike again. They were standing over a large, angled design board. The project paper was in front of them and they were trying to solve an issue of design space usage. Mike was a bit frustrated he hadn't found a solution yet.

Then God released the hounds of humor. Both men were standing over the document. Bob tapped his mechanical pencil on the table and said these words: "You know, Mike, this puzzle we're trying to solve is sort of like 'Bubbleen, Little Joe.'"

And then the three seconds of wonder I can barely wait to see once I get to heaven. I will ask to see it over and over and over again.

Mike turned his head, as on a swivel, leaned into Bob, and exaggeratedly mouthed, slowly and sternly, "What... did... you... say?"

Mike had not heard these words from outside his own head since 1983. His expression conveyed that if Bob did not say the exact words in response, Mike would choke him until he did.

Bob, in a moment of near genius said this: "Yeah, 'Bubbleen, Little Joe.' You know, from the *Bonanza* show. It's a statement people make when they hear something which doesn't make sense. You hear people in graphic arts use it all the time. It's like saying you've got a conundrum or a paradox of misunderstanding. You know, 'Bubbleen, Little Joe.'"

Mike stared at Bob like he had said, "Vegetable mallet of corrosive steam harnessing."

Mike: (moments of staring, then attempting to form words without success) "What?"

Bob: "'Bubbleen, Little Joe.' Come on, you know. Ben's trying to help Little Joe. And no one can figure out what he says next. Stop screwing with me. Now, let's get back at this."

Mike: (more trying to form words without success) "Where did you hear this? How do you know this? Nobody knows this. There's only one other person who..."

Then, mercifully, Bob smiled and said, "I know Lynch."

. . . Awakening . . .

God is able to stand in the pain and injustice,
while at once transcending it. He employs
humor, which reminds evil it cannot win.

, , , , , , , , , , ,

1995

THE SET WAS completely appointed for *Cappenetti's*, our next production, set in a local bar. It was magnificent! The warm wooden countertop, and overhead racks of wine glasses, framed by vintage-looking columns, filled nearly the entire back of the stage. Neon beer signs hummed, while diffused light from a series of ellipsoidal reflectors spilled down through the rack slats. Every conceivable libation was backlit prominently from behind where the bartenders would pour. Taverns in big-city gaslight districts wished they were this place.

We were opening in two nights. "We" were a theater troupe named Sharkey Productions. We had been painstakingly learning how to write and perform faith-based stories for the city that didn't offend sensibilities by bad writing and religious right turns. It might have been an easier endeavor for monkeys to type out *The Old Man and the Sea*.

We'd written a number of fairly mediocre plays our first several years, but recently, we were starting to find our footing.

The several dozen of us committed to this dream were having the time of our lives. For the first time, I discovered up close an intimate place where I was known, enjoyed, and needed. We laughed more than we rehearsed, and we rehearsed a lot. It was an immensely safe place to create and risk and fail and create again. We loved being together and were starting to learn to protect each other. This was one of the most enjoyable things I've ever done.

Several years later, we performed at the downtown prestigious Herberger Theater. But in 1995, we were performing out of our church. We remodeled the auditorium to look like a cool retro theater.

The crisis didn't dawn on me until the Sunday before we opened. I was sitting at church thinking, *Five days from now this stage will transform into a neighborhood tavern.* This would've been a marvelous thought when we only staged the plays for one weekend. But for the first time we were running two weekends. The set, complete with every imaginable alcohol and blaring beer sign, would be the decoration for our church services the following Sunday.

I know it's no big deal anymore. But at the time it was. Knowing what I know now about how this community sees community, faith, and buildings, I wouldn't have panicked. But I was still testing it all out, to see if it could be real. At that point, I'd been on staff for nearly five years. But this project was my deal. I'd tried to not give anyone reason to have issue with what we were doing. Now I was asking first-time visitors and alcoholics to show up and take communion in front of a fully functioning bar!

Sitting there, my issues with authority flooded back in: all the doubt, all the waiting rebellion. I was certain we'd have to tear it down and reconstruct it. I could've asked if we could drape it with canvas. No, that would've been stupid and weird.

Finally, I went to Bill.

"Yeah," he said. "I was thinking the same thing today. You won't be offended if I don't preach from behind the counter, will you?"

"What?"

"Look, this is a building. On Sundays, many of us who show up are probably God-followers. On Fridays and Saturdays, many might not be. God is happy to host both. It's a building. We don't violate anything by doing both. If sometimes the decor blurs together, I think folks will understand. If not, maybe we can help teach them or thank them for their time here. You're not covering that majestic set. We're so proud of you all. You're us. You represent us. I can't wait for opening night. I can't wait for the following Sunday. With our crowd, your biggest concern is people trying to sneak off with a shot of the good scotch after the service."

In those words, something ended in me. From that day on, I was never again waiting for the other shoe to drop. The sense I didn't belong—that who I am wouldn't fit in any church—it went away. In that moment, I knew when I failed, I wouldn't be asked to leave. I knew I would not have to eventually run. Ten thousand questions were answered with one response.

. . . Awakening . . .

We grow up wanting to be known,
and terrified we will be.

1995

I WAS SITTING in one of many repurposed military huts at the Gasinci Refugee Camp in northern Bosnia. It was a sticky June afternoon. Two brothers and their wives were slowly and quietly recounting for us the particular atrocities of the hell which had fallen upon Croatia, Serbia, and Bosnia the last half-dozen years. None of them made any noticeable facial expressions. They spoke in monotone. It was an eerie and heartbreaking experience to hear the one brother tell, without any emotion, of their third brother having his throat slit.

Everyone had walked with a suitcase or grocery bag many miles, through and around enemy checkpoints, to end up in this camp. We were the latest in a steady stream of well-intentioned caregivers to these war-displaced families. Every person we met could tell of a family member killed, tortured, or raped in this hideous ethnic genocide. No government is innocent, but most of these refugees were. They didn't want this war or cause this war. And now their own neighbors, with whom they had loved and done life, suddenly were enemies— burning homes and torturing old friends. A sick appeal to religious differences, national unity, and ethnic cleansing had demanded such.

I was worn down. This was our third day in the camp. Every story blended together. We were there to offer the hope of Jesus. But they were so wounded, so devastated, so full of shock and thinly buried rage, the offer of Jesus must've sounded like the promise of free accordion lessons.

"What you are offering might be nice in some other world, but right now we are awaiting news of how many family members are still alive and if we will be allowed to stay here another day."

I felt cheap. Listening to these couples, I realized I had come there with exceedingly wrong motives. I wanted to do something relevant and big for God. I wanted to go where there was the greatest need. I wanted to be in the center of the action. I wanted to have stories to tell of walking among the wounded in a war-torn country. I wanted to be the hip pastor who would go into harm's way. I wanted to come back home to our church with a report of the dozens who trusted Jesus.

The day before I had listened to a man who had watched his entire family cruelly killed, back home in Banja Luka. After listening to his story for a while, I tried to offer him the hope of Jesus. He shook his head slowly, back and forth. Through an interpreter, he said these words: "What do you want from me? I have lost my family. Where is God? And who is this new God you are trying to sell me? I don't want a God who would allow what I have seen. What do you want me to do? Would you like me to pray a prayer, so you can check off a list back home? I will do that. I did it for the last group. If I do it, would you then please leave me alone?"

I was embarrassed for the interpreter. I was embarrassed for myself. I excused myself and walked out of his barrack.

God, I want to go back home. I don't want to do this anymore. I don't like who I have tried to be—the great American, caring Christian. Help me. I don't know what to do. I have no relief gifts to offer. And You apparently are not what they are looking for at this moment. I don't know how to help. I feel trite and useless. Nothing seems strong or supernatural. It's like You aren't here. I hate this feeling. I'm so sorry to even think these words. I know You are here, but I have never felt oppression and darkness like I have these days. Help me fill the hours and get through this until we get on the bus taking us to the airport on Friday. I'm sorry I came here. I'm sorry I can't do anything. I'm sorry I'm misrepresenting You.

I wandered around the camp until early evening, when we all got into the van, back to the seminary in Osijek, Croatia, where we slept. Others were loudly recounting stories of hope and spiritual openness. I had nothing.

It was now Thursday morning. We made the drive back to the camp. I made the rounds with others to yet unvisited refugees, keeping a low profile. But it was too much to take.

I broke away from the group again to go outside and wander the camp. I noticed down in low-lying areas some even worse conditions. Apparently, even in refugee camps there are the haves and have-nots. I was informed this was where the "Roma" stayed. The Roma still live throughout Europe and the Balkans. I watched a deeply wrinkled, older man making impressive, intricate wooden spoons and vials. I offered to buy some. He was so appreciative. Eventually, I was asked into his family's "home." It was a stagnant, hot, dark room with no windows. The air was thick and full of sickness. A large hunk of unidentifiable meat sat on a table, flies devouring it. I so did not want to get sick. I wanted to excuse myself. But a man, perhaps in his late thirties, called out to me. He was seated across the room, crosslegged, on the dirt floor.

"You are from America, yes? So, why are you here?" He was clearly the leader of this family.

"Well, we're here to, um, offer comfort and, um, spiritual help to the people who have been through so much sadness."

"You're here to talk about Jesus, aren't you?"

"Well, um, yes. But we want to be sensitive to those who are not, um..."

"Tell me about this Jesus. Would you be so kind?"

For the next hour, we both talked, asked questions and answered, and asked some more. The room began to fill. They were leaning in and listening intently. I was suddenly willing to contract whatever was in this room. For the first time on this trip, I felt like Christ in John, being me. I was falling in love with humans from another continent.

When it was over, he asked if he too could be a Christian. He asked me what he must do. I led him through a rough, clumsy talk he could have with God about trusting what Jesus did at the cross and the resurrection. He prayed it out loud in front of everyone. Then he got up and hugged me.

He was smiling and so kind... He offered me the meat on the table. He saw my hesitancy, and we all laughed. Others hugged me. Jesus was fully there. He was there the other days. I couldn't see him, in the middle of my straining to prove myself. Why was this so different? I asked myself on the ride home. Maybe it was this: *Who I am, Christ in me, wants most to love. More than anything else. That's the real me.*

. . . Awakening . . .

*I am a lover on my worst day and misplace it only when
I pretend I have that which I'm not sure I really do.*

. . . .

I heard later he was baptized by someone from the group following us. Someday, at a wedding feast, in a land far away, we will meet again. And he will not be living in the bad part of town. He will be right in the middle of the city lit with the glory of God Himself.

1996

CALEB WAS TEN. Amy was eight. Carly was two. This piece ultimately comes from a conversation I had with God, one night spent on a couch, unable to sleep.

"God, am I seeing You correctly? Am I speaking about You in a way that glorifies You? I think I am. I teach that I can trust this new heart You've given me, and that I don't have to irrationally search for some deep, dark, wrong motive. Usually, I rest in that. But tonight I need to ask, You'd tell me if I'm way off on all I'm teaching about this identity and grace truth, right? You're giving me a larger audience. My kids and Stacey are being influenced by my way of seeing You. I can't find out later that I misrepresented You. Wait. Who am I kidding? I know the answer to what I'm saying. I know too much. I have learned to receive Your love. My life has been radically transformed, with a peace only You can bring. But I deceived myself so often before You. It's a groove that runs deep. Thank you, my God."

In the Old Testament, Israel largely knew God's power but not His person. They didn't have the new heart to obey yet. And so they rebelled, ran, returned, rebelled, ran, returned, rebelled, ran, and returned. Lather, rinse, repeat.

Then Jesus shows up on the scene. And suddenly we could see

God's person and not have to run or rebel! It still undoes me to write it. What must it have been like? Standing in the center of Jerusalem, hearing His words. Are you kidding me? What the human race had wanted forever had shown up in a body form they could touch. "Come to Me, all who are weary and heavy-laden, and I will give you rest. Take My yoke upon you and learn from Me, for I am gentle and humble in heart, and *you will find rest for your souls*. For My yoke is easy and My burden is light" Matthew 11:28-30 NASB (emphasis mine). And just like that, we didn't have to run from God anymore. We didn't have to perform, pretend or playact for God.

I was searching for a way to be able to say the convictions of my heart from God's perspective—to turn over all the cards and reveal His sweetest and deepest heart of love to us. I ended up calling the following piece "God's Great New Testament Gamble".

What if I tell them who they are?

What if I take away any element of fear in condemnation, judgment, or rejection?

What if I tell them I love them, and will always love them? That I can't love them more than I love them now; and I love them right now, no matter what they've done, as much as I love My only Son? That there's nothing they can do to make My love go away?

What if I told them they were righteous, with My righteousness, right now?

What if I told them they could stop beating themselves up? That they could stop being so formal, stiff, and jumpy around Me?

What if I told them I was crazy about them?

What if I told them if they ran to the ends of the earth and did the most unthinkable, horrible things—when they came back, I'd receive them with tears and a party?

What if I told them I don't keep a log of past offenses, of how little they pray, or promises made that they don't keep?

What if I told them they don't have to be owned by men's religious additions or traditions?

What if I told them if I'm their Savior, they're going to heaven, no matter what—it's a done deal?

What if I told them they had a new nature—saints, not saved sinners who should now "buck-up and be better if you were any kind of Christian, after all He's done for you!"?

What if I told them I actually live in them now? That I've put My love, power, and nature inside them, and it's all at their disposal?

What if I told them they don't have to ever put on a mask? That it's absolutely perfect to be exactly who they are at this moment?

What if they knew they don't have to look over their shoulder, for fear if things get too good the other shoe is going to drop?

What if they knew I will never, ever use the word punish in relation to them?

What if they were convinced bad circumstances are not My way of evening the score for taking advantage of Me?

What if they knew the basis of our friendship isn't on how little they sin, but how much they let Me love them?

What if they had permission to stop trying to impress Me in any way?

What if I told them they could hurt My heart, but I'd try to never hurt theirs?

What if I told them I like Clapton's music too?

That the "Thee's" and "Thou's" have always confused Me?

What if I told them I never really was that fond of the Christmas handbell deal with the white gloves?

That they could open their eyes when they pray and still go to heaven?

What if I told them it wasn't about their self-effort, but allowing Me to live My life through them?

176

. . . Awakening . . .

We are the test. Will seeing a God who is not angry at us, make us care less about the heart of God? Or, in realizing we are indwelt by the heart of God, will we find ourselves displaying heartfelt obedience and heartfelt, playful joy?

. . . .

On My Worst Day

1997

IN MOST OF my preaching, I don't usually give anyone anything specific to do with it. Others can do it skillfully and naturally, but I usually feel manipulative or hokey. I guess I've always thought God could direct people to do whatever He wanted them to do with what they were being taught. It's a nice-sounding theory, but in practice, it's a bit ridiculous. All areas of learning involve and include practical application. Jesus did it with His own teaching. I haven't known how to do it without coming off like a motivational speaker, selling soap in an ill-fitting shirt.

One Sunday I was speaking on 1 Peter 5:6–7: "Therefore humble yourselves under the mighty hand of God, that He may exalt you at the proper time, casting all your anxiety on Him, because He cares for you" (NASB).

"Casting your anxiety" has the idea of throwing a saddle over a horse, or hurling something with all your might. So I asked each family or individual to later try my clever little *action step*.

"Find a pillowcase and gather your family around your dirty-clothes basket. Have each of them think of something that creates anxiety or frightens them. Have them pull out an item of dirty clothing to represent that anxiety. Spend some time teaching how

God is able and longing to take it away if they cast it onto Him. Give each person a chance to tell their particular anxiety. Then let each person stuff their dirty clothes item into the pillowcase. Tie off the top and take your whole group out into your front or back yard. Take turns casting the pillowcase. Come back in to express what it was like throwing your scary thing into God's care."

My seminary preaching professor would have been so proud of me.

By the time the morning messages had been delivered, I'd lost interest in the whole exercise. But people would be expecting some kind of report about our family time on the following Sunday, so I had to try it out at home with our three children. At the time, Carly was four, Amy nine, and Caleb eleven.

Late one afternoon, I gathered us around the dirty-clothes basket in our bedroom. I had to admit, it went really well and it was a lot of fun. We were all into it. We laughed and talked about our fears, and prayed together. But, at the end of the day, I was mostly going through the motions, trying to host a God moment for my kids.

I'd forgotten all about it by the time I went in to lie down with Carly before bed. Twenty minutes later, I kissed her goodnight. Before I stepped out of her room, my little girl called out: "Dad?"

"Yeah?"

"They're gone."

"What do you mean? Who's gone?"

"The monsters. The ones who lived under my bed. The dirty clothes I put in that bag for Jesus to help me with. They're gone, Dad."

I was overcome in the doorway of her room. "Carly, that's incredible."

The hall light streamed into her darkened room, allowing her to see only my silhouette. She couldn't see my expression. I was wrecked.

I was witnessing God interacting with the trust of a human. My little girl had not yet learned to not trust God. She believed He would do something, sometime. She believed He had her back. He did. I know not everything plays out like this. But it shook me. Trust in His power, His rightness, His ability, His love, His control over every moment of our lives—it's not an option for us. Not at the start of the journey or any day after. Carly spoke of the monsters often before that day. She never spoke of them again.

In that moment, I was compelled to believe again what I'd forgotten. Somehow, in all the perfect, sovereign plan of God, some experience the magic of God because they trust Him to be able to do it. It freaks me out, but it's what He appears to promise. On that day, preacher man missed it, but his four-year-old daughter got it. She still gets it.

John, you can get information or knowledge from anyone, without almost anything on your part. But to receive wisdom, insight, discernment, or truth—ah, that will take trust. One can come simply through the brain. The other demands the heart's buy-in. To the extent you come under My words, trust My way of seeing, you will become wise. All around you are intelligent and knowledgeable people imagining they are wise. But they are only educated with what can prove them more right than someone else. They lack humility to trust another.

I will never fail you or play you. Come under My assessment, even when you don't understand or like it. You'll become wise. You have been hurt in these last few years. It has left you disillusioned and self-protective. This guardedness of your heart will leave you dry. If you don't let Me in, the wounded man will face his pain without wisdom and insight. This will create an even deeper pain.

John, allow your daughter to teach you tonight. This is no longer a preacher's gimmick. This is supernatural life, My dear friend.

I will become convinced that wisdom is the inevitable response to this:

- Trusting who Christ says I am, even when I don't feel worthy of it.
- Trusting who Christ says He is, even when He doesn't appear to be active in my experience.
- Trusting others with me, to protect me from my self-referencing madness.
- Trusting His Word, even when it doesn't portray the way I think God should be.

1997

IT WAS SO crowded at Squaw Peak Park that Saturday morning, I had to drive all the way to the top of the loop to find a parking spot. The peak itself was a steep, switchback hike, embedded with jagged rocks for me to trip over—to become the lead story on the five o'clock news.

"Hello, this is Kent Dana with Channel 10 News. Today, an

elderly, dehydrated hiker plunged down the western slope of Squaw Peak. In what took several hours, because of his fragile condition, paramedics eventually airlifted him out. Witnesses at the scene said he looked nearly incoherent before hurling headlong down the steep, cactus-strewn slope. We'll update you on his condition in a special report at ten."

I hated this hike. It offended me on so many levels. It shouted at me, "Hey, old-timer! I'm going to make you so miserable. I'm going to make you question your manhood... You're out of shape. You shouldn't be here. In the first quarter-mile we're going almost straight up. You'll be gulping for oxygen like you're on the moon. Little children will be passing you. You'll slug down your entire bottle of water before midpoint. And you'll create a rash from wearing Levi's. Did you think you were going to hike a furniture store?"

But Stacey wanted to hike it, so there we were. I was now walking down from the parking lot above. I had dropped her off at the trailhead, nearly half a mile down the same hill I would have to retrace later—after I am left dehydrated, rubbery-legged, and belittled by nature. I was in a bad mood as I wandered around in my head. At such times my head is a rough neighborhood.

I was complaining a steady internal whine. My whine was interrupted by this random thought: *My golf game is so bad I'll bet I could shank my drive from the Biltmore golf course into this park.*

The course is over a mile from where I was walking. But self-pity knows no distances.

Maybe fifteen steps after that thought, I looked down. There, directly in front of me, mostly buried in the clay dirt was a golf ball! And I was suddenly overcome.

There it was again. That presence. That overwhelming sense of Him. That invading and overarching experience of being gratefully swallowed in awe.

I knelt down to pick up the ball. It was covered in the mud of last week's storm. I cleaned it off the best I could. It was suddenly an iconic, visible, tangible expression of God's ability to meet me at any single moment. This ball was from Him, saying,

> *John, I am here. Last month, a boy grabbed one of his father's golf balls from the backseat of his family's car, from the same parking lot where your car sits. He rolled it down the hill and lost interest in it as it rolled across the road into this culvert, where you now stand. I not only let him decide to lose interest, I formed that random thought for you and directed your eyes down at the exact moment. Pretty cool, huh?*

I was undone and lost in whatever worship is. In that moment there was no pretense or overreaching words. I couldn't speak. I stood for several minutes, holding the ball, not willing to leave that moment with my God.

I found Stacey and told her about what had just happened. She gave me that slight head tilt that says, *My husband is a bit of a kook.* But I drove directly home after the hike, washed the ball off, wrote the date on it, and placed it on my office shelf. For the rest of my life, it will stay with me and remind me, draw me, hold me. I was not yet aware much was heading towards me that would bring nearly everything into question. But on that day, I was given this. I had that ball. Others have the Shroud of Turin or nails from an ark. But I've got this golf ball from God Himself.

. . . Awakening . . .

*God is not only out there, watching me. He is
in here, fully identifying Himself with me.*

,   ,   ,   ,   ,   ,   ,   ,   ,   ,   ,

He is doing this life with me; completely and uniquely living my
experience.

Love has gone this far.

On My Worst Day

November 5
1998

THIS WAS THE hardest story for me to write in the entire book. Please be aware it may be painful to read.

For us, it all began with Stacey watching our five-year-old Carly play in the front yard. She received a phone call from Dennis Martin, my brother-in-law. "David has just shot himself. We're on the way to the hospital."

David Lee Martin—Dennis Martin is his dad, Cindy Martin his mom, Kristen Nunley is his sister, and Michael Martin his brother. Stacey is his aunt and I am his uncle.

David took his life a week before his fifteenth birthday, on November 5th, 1998.

I pause and sigh.

This story is anyone's worst day.

Dennis, Cindy, Kristen, and Michael have allowed me to tell David's story in order to give others hope, clarity, comfort, perspective, peace, and to experience God's care. I'm not a therapist, I'm an uncle. So, please show me grace as I try to parse my way through descriptions and labels.

Having chronic depression or mental instability can make you feel like you are a unique failure, a mistake. Who can carry that? Parenting someone with chronic depression or mental instability can also leave you feeling like a unique failure and that you are not enough. Who can carry that? And if a son or daughter takes their life, parents can feel like something is uniquely wrong with their family. *How could we have not stopped it?* Who can carry that? Each of these are lies from the very source of evil. All of us came to this broken planet, the posterity of a fallen line. We all carry vestiges of the death the human race caused. All of us. For some, it is more visible and ultimately more devastating. But our mental health has nothing to do with how much we are loved, adored, or valued by our God. Some of the most beautiful love stories are between God and the exceedingly fragile. Maybe it's because the fragile know they are needy. And love is the meeting of needs.

David was extraordinarily fun, funny, insightful, knowable, bright, and eminently safe and cool to his family and friends—especially his dear friends, Emily and Mike K. He was an exceptional skateboarder and was becoming a good guitar player. He made people laugh. He could read through a façade. If it wasn't real, he didn't trust it. He loved and enjoyed his family deeply. They loved and enjoyed him deeply back.

Sometime around the age of thirteen, David's brain started misfiring. He didn't know what to say, or how to explain it—something was just off. He thought it would pass. He kept skateboarding, playing music, and doing what felt safe. Lack of motivation and grade changes at school became noticeable. He began losing interest in soccer, which he'd loved playing since the age of five. It was becoming too hard for him to keep up with homework and sports while also fighting off this anxious noise within him. At thirteen, who has the maturity to process suddenly garbled messages? It scared him. The

Martins soon all realized that David was clearly depressed. They got him to a psychologist who started him on an antidepressant medication. While certain antidepressants are helpful for adults, they can do more harm than good for an adolescent with a still-developing brain.

Initially, it seemed like David was making a turn. But soon he could no longer push back the irrational messages bombarding him. Days before everything broke loose, God gave David a marvelous gift. All of us need affirmation but to a young man spiraling away from normalcy, love and respect from your peers is nearly everything. In the middle of October, his classmates voted him homecoming prince. Less than a month before his death, God was saying to him, "David, your life has been well spent. You are loved, trusted, and known by your friends. I only wanted for you to see it."

At a school celebration one evening, David stared around a room of those who deeply valued him. Many will never experience such goodness in their entire adult lives. Then it all went very dark. The last three weeks were so painful for everyone. Adults have life perspectives to face strangeness. But how horrifying to be young and experience your mind betraying you. There was no more time to buy. The data was corrupted and his ability to decipher it was quickly fading.

David wrote this in a note found after he took his life. "I'm so sorry, but I can't take it anymore. I love Mom, Dad, Kristen, Michael, Emily, and Mike. And I love you too, God."

"I love you too, God." A young man, at the end, knows his God is not to blame. Sacred.

This family will never stop remembering and will never fully stop grieving. Such is the nature of love. They grieve on the week of his birthday and the week of his passing. Even on their own birthdays, grief is there. But, also, they find themselves smiling and laughing over memories. It's why they ask others to keep sharing stories. Because they don't want to forget a thing.

Some who are reading this may have a son or daughter battling disturbing thoughts and feelings beyond their control. Maybe the clumsy thoughts I've recorded here will give you words to help talk to each other, and, if necessary, pursue therapeutic action. This is not your fault. It is not their fault. This is not because you don't have a good enough family. Once you are free from those untruths, you may discover yourself more actively able to receive the love of God and others. Some reading this have lost a child and are in a listless haze, wondering if joy will ever return. God can feel distant because you don't know what a relationship with Him looks like now. The Martins would tell you it will take time to find life's new normal. And no one can tell you what that new normal should look like. There is a God who loves you and loves who you lost. This can sound hollow, for He was on watch when this happened. Many of us who have faced this have been given the grace to reconcile the unthinkable with these two truths.

First, He loves the one you lost more than everyone else combined does. And He loves your child as much as He's loved anyone who's walked this earth. Secondly, sometimes, God miraculously heals. And sometimes, mercifully, He does not.

God is infinitely powerful but must love us in a world filled with death and illness. We, as the human race, bought the original lie, and it poisoned the air we breathe. Jesus, bearing on a cross what we could not, will bring us to everlasting Life. The best honoring of a life is to live our remaining time to the fullest and to sacrificially love those who remain. Dennis and Cindy are no different than others. They suffered and still suffer. They went through all the stages grief throws out. But, by God's grace, they chose to trust the one who allowed their son to be taken. Either He is good and able or He is not God. And if He is not God, well then, how can anything make sense? So, the Martins and their family are testing if He's real because living a life that matters is contingent on God being fully good. Over time, for them, He has proven Himself. Glory to God, they each have lives that deeply matter; marriages, children, and purpose. It is awe-inspiring to watch. We all respond differently, and in different timing. This is what chapter fourteen of a twenty-four chapter book looks like. God knows where you are. Let Him love you. Let Him care for you. He did not take your child. He stands with you and over you in the middle of this grief, feeling it to the exact extent you are.

Finally, where is my place in this story? I was a preaching pastor who counseled hundreds. But when it came to my own relatives, at their greatest time of need, I froze and didn't know what to do. My brother-in-law Dennis needed me. But I couldn't, or didn't, love him well. Maybe this will help it all make sense...

My mom died a tragic death when I was in my mid-twenties. No one knew how to help me face that. I remember calling my dad, days after, crying, "What do I do? I'm not making it through this." He was so kind, but all he knew to tell me was to get some sleep and not to forget to eat. Maybe no one helped him face death. I determined on my own that I would survive.

No one knew how to walk me through my brother's mental illness and death. I think I involuntarily protect myself from shocking pain. I close off. I guess because I'm afraid I will go to a devastating place that I might not be able to return from. This is no excuse for not being there for those I love dearly, but it may help someone reading this to understand and be able to face their own similar story. It has taken me learning to trust God's strength and learning to trust others to begin to break this generational pattern. But my quiet broke Dennis' heart. We were distant for quite a while. But God's tenacious love has brought redemption. Dennis and I are dear friends again. Maybe closer than before.

A few weeks before the deadline of this book, David's story was still not included in the manuscript. And it dawned on me that one of my worst days had never been written about. This story. David's story. Dennis, Cindy, Kristen, and Michael's story. I met with Dennis to apologize. Then Cindy. Then Kristen and Michael. I asked if they would allow me to write the story now. What a gracious love for them to say, "Yes."

2001

I NEVER WANTED kids. They would get in the way of my dreams, my impact on the world. I wanted to be married to someone. Stacey only wanted kids. Apparently, I looked like I might be able to help provide her with kids. So she taught me how to love our children. Nothing since has been more important to me.

I know the absolute love of all three of my kids. They know only my accepting love and full commitment. I have given them each the best of me. They each play with me, make fun of me, and listen to how I see life. They affirm my life like I could have never possibly imagined—in notes, in public, in birthday letters of overwhelming affirmation.

My friend Norm Wakefield says he loves each of his kids most. "Dad, do you love me most?"

"Oh, yes. Absolutely. By far," he says the same to each of them. They get it.

Writing this, I love my youngest daughter Carly most. Amy and Caleb have fought with each other plenty growing up. But neither of them ever fought, argued, or got sideways with Carly. Who argues with someone kind, loving, and without much guile?

She would one day become our resident philosopher and biblical studies savant, understanding more theology, reading more books, and probably knowing how to exegete a text better than me.

I fear her best days will already be behind her. She peaked in this year. For she and I, over a nine-month period of time driving around in the car, created songs filled with free association. I will never forget a single lyric of them. God was gracious to give me a child who enjoyed the bizarre non-sequitur nearly as much as I.

Here's a sampling of the songs coming out of that season with my eight-year-old.

"The River Goat"
Hey, hey, the River Goat.
The River Goat's on our team.
The River Goat, the River Goat,
The River Goat's on our team.

"A Bucket of Squirrels"
A bucket of squirrels my friend is now.
A bucket of squirrels my friend is now.
A bucket of squirrels my friend is now,
He's not one to bake a cow.
A bucket of squirrels my friend is now.

"A Water Buffalo"
I wish I was a water buffalo,
I wish I was a water buffalo.
For if I was a water buffa,
I would be so very tougha,
I wish I was a water buffalo.

And this potential Broadway tune:

"Keplinger"
Keplinger, Keplinger, he's a mouse.
Keplinger, Keplinger, where's your house?
Keplinger, Keplinger, don't be a louse.
Oh, find your way in the—
Find you way in the—
Find your way in the world.

...Cholesterol plaque may now take me at any time. My work here is largely done.

On My Worst Day

2002

THERE ARE MOMENTS when God shows His hand. When they happen, I find myself apologizing for every moment I've doubted His character, plan, and love. On this night, my family was in Tucson, at the University of Arizona, watching Caleb run the 800 meters in the Arizona high school state finals.

He had been a distance runner since seventh grade. But something changed late in his sophomore year. He started running the anchor on Washington High's 4x800 relays. The last four races, he'd been running down some very good runners in the last lap. He actually qualified at regionals to go to the state meet. It was now an hour before race time. I was more nervous than when I ran at Camp Oaks. Caleb was not. He knew why he was running. He wasn't owned by what drove me. When I grow up, I want to be like my son Caleb. There is something so overwhelming and humbling to be a father who starts a line of faith in a family. I'm still stuck in a bunch of generational patterns my family line passed on. But now I was watching my children, healthier than me, thriving because of the faith I've passed on to them.

I was bent over, behind the stadium bleachers, with a growing sense I might be momentarily throwing up my concession-stand nachos.

There was something about that night that felt disproportionately important. It shouldn't have. Caleb was a sophomore. He'd be running against some of his great heroes—legends of Arizona middle distance running. Matt Burton had already won State in this race before. It would have been notable for Caleb not to finish last.

I started begging God. This was not prayer. It was a father's full-on, selfish begging. *Father, protect my son. I know he can't win, or even place, but let this be a heroic night for him, where he gets to see Your hand...*

Forget that! Do something supernatural. Let him find a way to stand on that podium. There I said it. I think I'm going to vomit.

Wait. One more thing. My dad's here. He's starting to drift away with dementia. I would love for him to see Caleb run the race of his life. So, there. I'm begging. Don't let tonight hurt him. Being a father is so hard. I find myself caring more than I ever have and now absolutely unable to help.

Okay. I really am going to vomit now.

At the starting line, he looked like a boy lined up against full-grown men who'd already financed their own homes. He was terribly thin. He filled out his uniform like a lizard wearing a suit coat.

The race began. Caleb was on the inside lane, and immediately got boxed out. He looked passive, like he was frightened to be in such a field. He tried to make a move but was quickly trapped inside. As he ran by us on the first lap he broke free and rushed up on the pack. I'd seen this before. He started sprinting too early. His heart was bigger than his endurance. He was very fast but could fade at the end if he gave too much too early. Predictably, on the backstretch, Matt Burton stepped into another gear and burst out to a twenty-yard lead.

Then, on the backstretch, Caleb made a decision to go after him.

He later told us what was going through his mind in those moments—that all he could think was: *Okay, God, I think this is going to hurt—a lot. Thanks for getting me to this moment. Cover me. I'm going to make a move with all I've got. Here we go.*

In moments, Caleb worked his way through the pack and was actually making a move on this modern-day centaur. No matter what happened now, even if he faded to the back of the pack, Caleb had broken a family-line pattern of fear. He had risked greatness and not pulled back into less painful safety.

By the final turn, he sprinted up even with Burton. The stands erupted at this unexpected turn of events.

What was a coronation had now become a race.

It was hard to comprehend what I was seeing from my son! *What is he doing?*

I realized Caleb was not just trying to make the podium. He actually thought he could win this!

The last stretch was where Burton had buried the hopes of dozens of very good runners. They'd be lulled into thinking they're in the race, and then he'd steadily pull away, with his refined form and strong, long strides.

Caleb's form was starting to break down as he reached deep for his final seventy yards. Accumulated lactic acid was surging through his body. He was visibly contorted and locking up.

I'd suffered this scene before. Caleb would fall short. We would all congratulate him afterward on a great effort. But he would fall short. That's how life plays out for most of us.

But then, shockingly, with fifty yards to go, Caleb was still hanging on to him… like a shredded flag in a hurricane.

Nearly everyone in the stadium was now standing. It was like they knew the outcome, but wanted to honor the courage of both runners.

It was thunderously loud around me. With twenty yards to go, this was no longer about who was the better, stronger runner. This was about something else entirely.

The last ten yards will be forever etched in my mind. He looked behind by at least a step. He was lunging more than running.

Caleb then displayed what he had recently discovered, but had yet to risk in such competition: He had another gear.

Still twisted and gasping, his strides were even with Burton. And with one more shockingly fast stride, he leaned forward... and hit the tape first!

The crowd around me was wild with stunned delirium! Stacey, next to me, was moaning a crying yelp, blended with a guttural howling. I looked over at her. We both were crying. I scanned over to see my father. He was three rows in front of me. Instead of taking in all the hoopla in front of him, he turned back to stare at me. I had never before seen him make this open-mouthed, stunned, ear-to-ear smile. Late in the night, with everyone asleep in our Tucson hotel room, I laid in bed with our video camera propped on my chest. In the dark, I watched the race over and over—to make sure it had still actually happened.

John, there is funny and then there is you under those bleachers. One of the perks of My job is I get to see wonderful moments no one else does. And I get to create moments like that frozen stare between you and your father. That too, was prepared from before the world began. I have many more such moments coming. This life is hard. It will get harder. But My extravagant love does not begin in heaven. I love you in the now.

Oh, about Caleb. You know he wasn't supposed to win that race, right? Ninety-nine times out of a hundred, he wouldn't have. But what he said to Me on the backstretch—it over-whelmed Me. I am undone at such daring trust.

On My Worst Day

2003

BOB RYAN AND I were in Tempe this one evening. With three hundred others, we were packed into a bar named Gibson's, waiting for the concert to begin. Bob and I had co-written most of the scripts for Sharkey Productions over the years. He became one of my closest friends. He's the most gifted writer and songwriter I know. Brilliant, well read, and exceedingly funny, he may understand Flannery O'Connor and Bob Dylan better than they understand themselves. In the '70s, his folk-rock band was being groomed for a contract with Asylum Records, until drugs did him in before the band could make it into the studio. He can sing all the harmony parts to "49 Bye-Byes" and still writes and records exceptional music informed by that era.

He would tell me the truth about my preaching. He cared enough to call me out on my nonsense. He enjoyed and understood my particular gifting as much as anyone I know. He has stayed close to me when others have run off.

And he was an absolute mess. He had lived for decades with a deep, abiding faith in Jesus and carried a heavy backpack of compulsions, obsessions, and addictions. He represents millions. Maybe he represents all of us. I know there is an entire strain of Christendom which teaches such dissonance cannot exist in a "real" believer. But

I choose to walk with his deeply dependent faith over a crowded, shiny ship full of pietistically, self-managed strivers. So will God.

As a young pastor, with no small Messiah complex, I used to believe I could help "fix" Bob. I couldn't. I can't. Eventually, in some ways, he will probably be more of my teacher than I will be his. Bob has clumsily trusted God for any health he carries. Such is the astounding beauty given to those who stay in community long enough.

. . . Awakening . . .

All untested religious answers get tested over time. Only what is from love remains.

, , , , , , , , , , ,

This is when the wisdom of dependence and humility begins to reign. Friends stop posturing and become real to each other.

He and I have gone through so much there is very little pretense anymore. Ten years later, when I first set out to write this book, it was his voice I most needed to hear. We set aside several days and headed north. We sat on a cabin's deck, overlooking the forest surrounding Prescott. I asked him what he thought of my idea to write this book. He puffed slowly on his cigar and said: "John, you're not nearly as good a writer as you are a speaker. When you speak, you have this supernatural God-presence thing. When you write… not so much. You will have to be you. Don't write to make a point you think you should. Don't bully people you disagree with. Sometimes, on your blogs, you go after an enemy I'm not even sure exists. Write what you want to write and only that. If you don't represent these truths with the natural, unforced story of your life by now, you probably haven't believed it anyway. Tell your story. Don't prove anything. Who knows? Maybe some of the stories will be salvageable to perform on the road. That's where you're best."

See what I mean?

Anyway, that evening back in 2003, we were seeing Bruce Cockburn in concert. Bob had introduced me to his music ten years before. If I could see only one more concert before I leave the planet, it would still be Cockburn. He's a Canadian with a slightly better following than retired bull rider Bobo Gleason. He's spanned five decades, playing a combination of folk and rock which seems created exactly for me. He's angry, while profoundly and tenderly hopeful.

He's a God-lover. You wouldn't catch it by much of his music. But some of the most transcendent words about Jesus I've ever heard were penned by him. For me, with few exceptions, those considered "Christian artists" carry some measure of synthesized feel to their music. I know that sounds smug and immature. But what Bob told me about writing is true about music. Those who aren't trying to prove anything prove the most. How many lines are better than "fascist architecture of my own design"? Or "you tore me out of myself alive"?

Cockburn would play this song in the next few minutes. He wrote it back in the '80s. I would stare—transfixed and closer than usual to my place in the universe. The song would be the anthem for the rest of my journey.

2003

IT WAS FEBRUARY 16th. I was sitting on a stool on the back patio at the Encanto restaurant in Cave Creek. Stacey had been planning this fiftieth birthday party a long time. I had chosen to celebrate my birthday by taking this occasion to list and describe the hundred greatest influencers of my life. Many of them sat around the neighboring tables.

It would be the last time I'd have this large a gathering for a birthday. I was as much in the middle of community life as I would ever again be. I'd be known much more outside my little world not long from then. But I didn't yet realize how deeply I'd miss this group, which would change and grow smaller over the next decade.

I'd asked for there to be no affirmation time tonight. Such had been done for me, in astonishing measure the last twenty years, more than for anyone I knew. My friends would each come with written notes that I'd cry my way through before bed early in the morning. Tonight was to affirm them, to affirm our community, our way of life. I was in the middle of a predestined moment—to bless not only those at the tables but all who had been part of this improbable journey to grace. I was fully in the moment, fully made for that moment, fully a part of it, fully undone simply in the affirming of these lives who had helped save my own. Stacey had arranged for Steven Larson to share a hilarious piece he wrote, mocking my every idiosyncrasy. He is one of my all-time favorite humans, and perhaps the funniest person I know. He wouldn't let up. All of us were laughing like hyenas, filled with helium, gasping for breath.

At some point, a song was played. I looked around the gathering and got lost in this thought: *You took this chameleon, who never felt known, and You let me be known. With no pretense, no props. These people have seen the worst and best of me. They value me and allow me to influence them. How do I thank You for this? This evening feels about as good as this life will ever be able to get. You saw this too, didn't You? You put this together, with all my tastes, desires, and favorite moments. You knew exactly what I'd want.*

I imagine God replying,

Drink it in, kid. I'm sitting in the back, watching every moment. This is what I could see the evening Arlene broke up with you. You have no idea what your seventieth birthday will be like. Oops! Shared more than I probably should have. "Waiter, another glass of Syrah, please."

2003

AMY AND I were sitting in my car, up on the mountain again. Same pattern each time. I'd buy her a chocolate shake from Wendy's and we'd drive, north of Lincoln and Thirty-Second Street, until we were overlooking the city. I'd ask a few questions. She'd give short, begrudging responses. We'd sit some more. When I'd realize it wasn't going anywhere, I'd drive us back down the hill. This was drive number six.

I wasn't sure what else to do.

Amy had been hiding her life from us—going to bed when we did and then slipping out later to the computer, entering conversations she knew we'd fight her on. She was becoming more closed off. She'd been fighting everyone's protection of her and hiding communications from a world she didn't want us to know about. Now, she had pulled away. I never wanted this in my family. I thought I'd done everything to prevent it. I found myself going into "cop" mode, where I'd make ultimatums and threats of loss of privileges. I hated this. I never wanted to be that dad.

I think she wasn't opening up to me because she wasn't sure she could trust me. I'd been pretty absent for a while now, buried in my own aspirations. Amy paid the most of anyone for the absence of my emotional presence. She was forced to figure things out herself, to come to her own conclusions, formed in isolation.

I was only now seeing it. I desperately tried to earn my way back into a trust that could protect her heart. She wanted it so much but did not want to be fooled again. She couldn't tell if my sudden attention was because I was doing the good Christian dad thing, or because I adored her with everything in me.

Today's approach was different. I had no agenda. I wanted my daughter to know my sorrow, my apology, my commitment. I was tired of fighting her. I wanted back in so badly. After a few minutes of silence, I blurted out: "Amy, I don't know if you believe me yet. But I would give up everything I am or can do. I'd move our family to Grass Valley and deliver mail to convince you of my love. I don't have anyone in the world I love more. No one. I will do anything to convince you I want to be your fan, your protector, your hero. I will not lose you, my daughter. I'm so sorry I've been so self-consumed. You needed me, and I wasn't there. It will not happen again."

That day she melted. She believed me. She opened up and poured out her sadness. She let me back in. For the next year, we'd meet almost every week for coffee before school. We'd go through Proverbs, 1 Peter, 2 Timothy, John. Mostly, we'd talk—about everything and anything. She was listening to me in a way I had never been listened to. I was listening in a way I'd not listened before. I was getting to be a father in a way my father had longed for with me.

One afternoon, months later, I asked Amy for her keys so I could put her new registration form into her car's glove box. I opened the door and there, taped all across her dash, were 3-by-5 cards, with verses and quotes from our times together. I stood, transfixed, at that dash for a long time... My daughter had been drinking it all in all along. She wanted to live out the life her father was trying to describe. I came into the house, not knowing what to say. She was sitting on the couch, staring at her laptop. *Had she thought about me seeing those cards when she gave me her keys?* I chose to not say anything and she didn't seem to be waiting for my response. I sat near my daughter, smiling, as I thumbed through a magazine.

. . . *Awakening* . . .

My children desperately need me to own my failures;
it allows them to trust me so they can express their
own pain, vulnerability, and best moments.

. . . .

On My Worst Day

2008

IT HAD BEEN several weeks since I'd returned from the eleventh annual "Ernest Borgnine Memorial Music Appreciation Society" weekend. A long way back, about fifteen of us, all good friends and addicted lovers of music, decided we would get together several times a year to share our favorite pieces with each other. We needed a name. Someone tossed Ernest's name into the mix. It seemed to fit. An actor, who'd been in film and television for over half a century. I think we liked the name and the fact that he seemed to be such an affable, approachable personality. So, for over ten years we'd been getting together, usually arriving with burned CDs, each with thirty to forty-five minutes of music representing our lives.

To begin each event, we'd play the theme music from *McHale's Navy* while a giant smiling placard of Ernest sat in front of us. On our turn, we each usually gave some introduction, explaining how we were doing, often including extensive printed packets of lyrics, pictures, artist biography, or our own written reflections on why we picked our particular music. It was a sacred and sometimes absurdly wild time. We prayed for each other. Someone usually played their own music. There was always great food, cigars, and a featured wine pairing by the resident bartender. During each man's "set," no one would get up or speak much at all, respecting each other's offerings. Our tenth year was the culmination.

Several had gotten the idea of writing to Ernest and letting him know what we did. We knew we risked freaking him out—seventeen grown men playing music in front of a placard drawing of him.

But we thought it was worth the risk.

He received the email and his agent communicated he'd be honored to see us. So, several of us flew out to his home in Beverly Hills. He was so touched that several months later he boarded a plane to join us for our tenth annual event!

We each included a song on a compilation CD we had made for him, sharing why his unbridled joy and self-effacing ease made him the perfect fit for our yearly shindigs. One of us had created artwork on the CD and on the matching t-shirts, bearing his smiling mug. He danced, laughed, and sang to the music. I read a story of his life I had prepared. We listened to his stories about Lee Marvin and Betty Grable. He let us call our parents and he talked to them! It was a rare and marvelous weekend.

Late the first evening, he stunned us with these words: "Gentlemen, I've been honored all my life for what I've done. How incredible, at this stage of my life, for the very first time, among men half my age, I would be honored for who I am." He shook his head from side to side and then down. None of us spoke for a long while.

. . . Awakening . . .

Affirmation heals and humbles and makes me
want to do more of what I'm being affirmed for.

. , . , . , . , . , . ,

On Sunday morning, after we each had prayed for him, in front of him, he cried and said, "If church was anything like this, I think I'd come all the time."

On My Worst Day

2010

STACEY AND I awoke on this morning in Santorini, Greece. A deeply generous couple had sent us on a once-in-a-lifetime trip for our twenty-fifth anniversary. How much we spent was of little issue to them. We'd been gallivanting around the globe like wealthy retired people—from Paris to Bordeaux, Venice to Tuscany, and now Greece. We took the hour-and-a-half gondola ride in Venice—just because we could.

That morning, we found ourselves sitting next to a Jewish couple in our elegant restaurant at our elegant hotel. The food was so good, I wanted to stuff cheese Danishes into my pockets. Over the next hour, this couple became our friends. We were invited to join them on a tall-sail dinner ship, which would drift from one white-bleached-building-covered island to another, as the sun slowly painted the sky deep red. On the ship, we met another Jewish couple. Within minutes we were all laughing and yakking, like we'd known each other all our lives.

They wanted to know our story. I didn't want to tell them. I didn't want to ruin the evening and our friendship by telling them I was a Christian speaker and writer. I'd seen how this plays out. I usually sense it's my responsibility to make sure they heard the Gospel. I almost always feel like I'm selling soap to people who were moments before risking to trust me. They'd feel betrayed and confused. And I'm left with a bad taste in my mouth.

The couples persisted. They must hear all about us. After Stacey and I briefly explained our lives, they were full of questions. Not defensive questions. Honest and vulnerable ones.

In a moment, I decided to see where God was taking this evening. *I am a Christian. They know who I am.* Tonight, I would not proselytize. I would love and be loved. I caught Stacey's eyes and realized she was good with taking a similar tack.

The next several hours were filled with life. We had marvelous talks about everything: parenting, marriage, love, failure, regret, periodontics, books, my book, the Cleveland Indians. We were enjoying each other with such honest freedom.

The man from the couple we had met at breakfast took me aside. "I almost always feel disrespected and devalued by Christians. Like I have no faith, or my faith is all wrong. I want to tell them, 'You know your guy is from our team, right?' Anyway, you aren't doing that to me. Thank you. I know you're probably struggling with this, thinking you should be saying more. But I already know what you would say. I've heard the message from Christians so often. Here's something you may not know I see. Most of us see it; I know you Christians have something. I really do. I'm incredibly intrigued. You're giving me tonight a chance to test out what I'm seeing without being clubbed like a baby seal. Thank you."

Stacey and I had decided earlier that when the ship docked we'd walk up the steep, ancient donkey path leading up from the sea to this cliff-carved town. The two couples had already decided to take a gondola to their hotel. We were halfway up the path, pausing to watch the Mediterranean Sea reflect the moon. Then we heard voices. They were calling our names. It was our Jewish friends! They had run up the steep path to catch up with us. They were fully out of breath.

"Hey, we couldn't do it. We didn't want the night to end. We didn't want to stop seeing you. Would you guys let us buy you drinks? There's an outstanding bar at the top, overlooking an incredible view below. They serve the best Mojitos on this continent."

Within minutes we were sitting together in the bar, leaning back on comfortable cushions, overlooking lit pools and patios below us and the moon above us on this open-air pavilion. It was all majestic, serene, and otherworldly. The climb and the humidity had made us all desperately thirsty. I was slurping down Mojitos like they were ice teas. I'd never been in a moment where people with such radically different faith were so honest about their doubts, wonders, and dreams of how we hope life turns out. In trying not to force the Gospel, I'd unwittingly given the Gospel in a much more loving and comprehensive way than maybe I ever had.

It was now 2:45 a.m. I was officially drunk. I hadn't meant to be. But I was. We all hugged and made promises about vacations we would take together. Then my loopy chick and I maneuvered our way through the streets and alleys of ancient Santorini, feeling very much like savvy locals.

The next morning I asked Stacey, "What happened last evening? Did you feel all right about our conversations? Even when they asked me directly, I didn't want to give them the formula. I wanted to let Christ love them through me. To allow myself to be loved by them. Part of me feels like I let God down for not closing some deal. But a much larger part of me feels good. We all need God. They don't need Him more than me. Every day I need the redemption and healing of Jesus. I wanted them to know that. I guess I'm counting on this conversation continuing. But last night was so beautiful to me. I don't know when I've ever loved people who don't believe our faith, the way I get to love people who do."

The old order of John Lynch—pious, religious man—had been changing for a long time. But what happened that evening revealed it to me. People are not unwitting candidates for my speeches about God. They have profound dignity. They carry the image of God. God is sovereign. I know there may be a time to explain more, but that night had not been it. I think He likes it when I'm not manipulating conversations to get to the bonus question.

I was three continents over, being taught by Jews how to be a Christian. Shalom.

2011

FISHING IS ITS own reward—if you catch a fish, all the better. But every once in a while, if the morning clouds have formed a blanketing canopy above you—and everything is just right—God gives you an incomparable gift as a reward for getting up early: the experience of the dawn bursting open above you. Gleaming light of yellow, crimson, and orange rain down on you like a piñata just cracked open. And if that wasn't grand enough, the yet undisturbed surface of the lake creates a mirror image, so your entire world is awash in flaming color. Everyone near you is brightly lit as you are piloted transcendently in a Christmas tree color wheel.

A dear friend, Nadine Houston, took a picture of a scene just like that from the deck of their home situated over a lake. It was one of those rare times when a picture did the memory justice. Next time you see me, ask me to show it to you on my phone.

On one particular morning, I was fishing on Grand Lake in Oklahoma with friends. Such a canopy had formed over us. I was involuntarily yelping out, "Lord Jesus, Son of Mary, thank You! You are so good. Why would You do this for us?! Hallelujah!" My friends were doing the same. Only in their minds.

I had fished over a hundred times. With my dad at a stocked

fishing pond; with a good friend Jim, in Oak Creek Canyon near Sedona; with a girlfriend's dad, in the White Mountains of Northern Arizona. I've trolled for bass at Lake Powell while attending elder retreats. I've fished for trout with my son in Colorado's Sangre De Cristo mountains. Most often, I've fished by myself, with a cheap Zebco rod and reel. Like the one I laid across the bumper of my 1960 VW, to prop open the back hood enough so it wouldn't vapor lock.

Let me make this clear to you up front; I am not a good fisherman. I do not have good touch once the bobber moves. I do not know how to set a hook. I do not have good skills to keep a fish on the line. I do not know how to bring a fish into the boat. I do not know how to fish. I prayed to catch fish long before I believed in God. I blame my lack of skill on my dad, along with my ineptitude at all things home improvement and automotive. It is a fair blame. Dad would smile and agree.

It was June 22nd, 2011. I was 58 years old. On this particular fishing expedition in Oklahoma, the five of us were split up between two guides. Three were placed with the primary guide in his shiny, bass championship, award-winning boat. They were all comfortably situated with gear, sandwiches, and all manner of provision. Then their shiny, award-winning, bass boat, with its Mercury FourStroke motor, loudly gurgled an intimidating exit.

Jeff Hutsell and I were shown to our much less impressive, three-person, flat-bottom bass boat. Jeff and I barely knew each other at that time. In the coming years, he ended up becoming a close, trusted friend. He's a wonderful man who always carries an underlying guiding intention: for Jesus to be seen through him.

As we got ready to head out on the water, I didn't have the heart to tell Jeff that whenever I don't catch fish, those with me rarely do either. It's like a curse for something I must have done early in life. I don't even believe in curses but how else do you explain this?

We were introduced to our guide. His name was Hank. Hank was old. His arms looked like burnt leather, conditioned with oven grease. Hank mumbled as a form of speech. He probably wanted to be stuck with us no more than we wanted to be stuck with him. We wanted to catch fish. He looked tired, disoriented, and unsure of where the engine cord might be located.

We were handed poles with bait. We ventured a few hundred yards out into the lake. Hank turned off the engine. All, for a moment, was quiet. Then, casting. And more casting. And more casting. And, of course, no fish. I knew this familiar rhythm. I played along, like we were casting for a reason.

Jeff began asking Hank questions about his life. I wasn't at all interested in Hank's life at that moment. I just wanted to catch a fish. Eventually, Jeff asked Hank why he was a guide. Hank shyly mumbled something about bass championships. Bass champion- ships?! The ones on network television? Oh my gosh! They are an incredible spectacle these days. The winner gets a boatload of cash, a huge ceremony with fireworks, and the keys to a new boat handed to you by Miss Louisiana.

In Hank's bass championship days, there was no money... and no Miss Louisiana. You got a boat, a sandwich, and a slap on the back from your competitors. It turned out Hank had won nearly a dozen of those early championships. Wow! We were sitting in a boat with the Babe Ruth of bass fishing! By this time, Hank's starting to almost like us; enough, at least, to offer us each a soft drink. Then, he started the motor. Above the hum, he smiled at us and mumbled what Jeff and I now quote each and every time we tell this story:

"Boys, there's a limestone quarry 'cross the way. I've taken dozen groups up there. Nobody's caught nothin'. Nothin'! But one day they's gonna show up. I know it. Someone's gonna catch a lotta white bass. Anyway, it's not like you're gonna to do worse than you are right here."

Soon, we settled in over a limestone quarry. My confidence level was a 2 out of 10. While adding new bait to our lines, Hank nonchalantly mumbled, "Boys, let's try bouncin' your bait off the bottom." *Bounce my bait off the bottom?!* I thought. *Have we just given up? I may not be a good fisherman. But I'm not stupid. I am not bouncing bait off the bottom.* I, instead, continued spin casting.

At the other end of the boat, there was a sudden, chaotic commotion. Jeff had caught a fish. Then another. And another. As fast as he could reload. Incredulously, I ask, "Jeff, are you bouncing your bait off the bottom?!" Between laughs and gulps of air, he gets out, "Yes, I am! John, they're going crazy!"

In one of the top two sporting decisions I've ever made, I began bouncing my bait off the bottom. Before I could start to reel in, I had a bass. A huge bass! Hank grinned and slapped his knee. "Well, I'll be! I knew they's comin'. Here, son, let me get some bait on that there pole. We's about to have some fun."

In twenty-five of the most hilarious and outrageously fun minutes of nearly my entire life, we pulled in seventy or more, beautiful, sizable white bass. And as we did, we called out, "Come on, Hank! Pull it together, old fella! More bait. More bait! This is not a rehearsal." Hank smiled like Miss Louisiana had just handed him the keys to a brand new boat.

I felt like Peter with John and Jesus on the Sea of Galilee. Well, I mean, if Peter and John were in the same boat. And if Hank were Jesus. But as I pulled in another, I did feel the presence of Jesus, behind me, laughing hard, right in our midst. I didn't have time to understand it. I was too busy enjoying the moment with every fiber of my being.

We laughed and yelled so loud that the others could hear us across the lake. They soon joined us. At first, their boat was motionless and still, while ours rocked like a fraternity pontoon craft.

Soon enough though, our friends and their guide began bouncing bait off the bottom. And in no time, we were all laughing and trash-talking—in the best and kindest way. We ended up catching enough fish to feed Peru for a day or two. Most were caught and released, but many were cleaned for a feast later at the shoreline home of our delightful hosts, the Houstons.

When the fishing was done, and we headed back to land, I stood on the dock, watching Hank clean my fish. I had misread Hank. I've misread a lot of people. I judge them. And instead of ever making me pay for it, God gives me an astonishing gift: His kindness that brings me back to a right way of thinking—His way of thinking. That day was not a coincidence of fate. I experienced God's kind, intentional, playful favor.

In time, I settled back into my inability to catch fish. But whenever Jeff and I see each other, our first smile is about the memory of that day. Jeff called the guide company recently to inquire about Hank. He's still alive, but no longer works as a guide. I guess once you've taken folks on a search for the Holy Grail and found it for them, well, your work is mostly done. *Enjoy your days, Hank. Keep telling folks at the community center about those two nice men you were able to convince to bounce their bait off the bottom of a lake. Though most may think it's just another fishing story, that one actually happened.*

. . . Awakening . . .

All of life is a gift. But when God gives a specific gift, it is to communicate His love and my worth. If I am paying attention, it gives me a sense of my place in the world.

. . . .

2012

I REMEMBER HOLDING Caleb as a baby, thinking, *God, I'm counting on this way of life in grace to work for him. This feels like a huge risk. Am I right to raise him this way? I want him to grow up in such safety, freedom, and life that he will never have to rebel. I want him to know who he is in Jesus so strongly that his new nature will guide him to obedience, rather than religious compliance. I want him to never have to fake it or pretend an expected life. I want him to know the power of God to mature him from the inside out. I want it all to be so real to him. I want him to be closer to God than I am.*

Then came Amy... and Carly. We were a family, trying out this way of life in grace. I was falling in love with being a dad. I watched Jesus make our faith real in front of our kids. Each of them were gradually coming to trust Him on their own. It was hard to believe that this man who had run from God for so long was having the privilege to help raise a family in such health and love.

I remember one particular vacation, all together in Laguna Beach. One afternoon, I was videotaping my children playing in beautiful Shaw's Cove. And it all suddenly flooded back to me, right while I was filming: that Laguna Beach chapter—my last-ditch effort at fighting off God's pursuit. I could actually feel the pain of how hard I tried to prove I was someone worth loving. And now, transposed over those scenes, were my own children, occupying the exact same space. With the camera running, I started crying, and could not stop... In a box in our attic is a five-minute clip of two-year-old Carly being knocked over by waves, laughing with her big brother, sister, and mom, while her dad is blubbering into the camera about God's redemption.

It all gradually caused me to want to offer this way of life to others. Most of my friends didn't grow up in families like this. I didn't grow up in a family like this.

As the kids got older and I watched them choose behaviors from trusting this life in Christ, I began to realize, "It works. This way of life in grace, it works!"

I wanted my family, our community of families, to be able to counter the prevailing theology that children brought up in grace would take advantage of it, to live a double life.

I was watching a theory of grace become a tested experience. It was astonishingly beautiful.

And then it all seemed to unravel in a single phone call.

Almost from the start, Amy's marriage had been hard. But I didn't know how hard. None of us did. Now, less than two years in, she was losing hope. We knew she was withdrawing. We just didn't know how to help. Her husband didn't want our counsel or help. So, we tried to give them room to work things out.

Amy is one of the finest humans I know. She is our kin-keeper. She is beautiful, thoughtful, and playful. She is funny and plays with people on their terms. Nobody has written more astoundingly undoing letters of affirmation to me.

That's partly why I was so devastated by the phone call.

Caleb called, having just talked to Amy's husband. Stacey blurted out the "f" word. My wife had never used the word before. I think in that moment, I went into a form of shock. I innately knew, whatever was just said, would change our family forever. Something precious had just fallen from my hands and shattered onto the floor.

Stacey got a hold of Amy. She told her she'd been hiding from us her involvement in a wrong relationship with another man. For some time.

"What! What does that mean? Who, when, uh, let me talk to her."

"She hung up. She doesn't want to talk right now. She wants to be alone."

"But, but, I'm her dad. I have to talk to her."

I dialed her phone number twenty times in five minutes.

That night I laid in bed, churning and playing, over and over, questions that had no answers: *What do I do now? God, help me. What do I say to her? How did this happen? Oh, God. I feel like I can't breathe. How do I protect Amy? How do I let her know I love her while I'm still trying to figure out how she got to this place? Should I call her husband? He doesn't want to hear from me. But I should call him. Help me, God. Why wouldn't she want to talk to me? I've been through everything with her. Should I get in the car and drive out to California?*

The damage was too devastating. Their marriage ended months later.

Amy came back home from California. Our community swung into action to love her. She began to face what had happened. She was incredibly heroic. She went to college full of innocence and hope. Now she was trying to unravel what had happened so quickly. She was bravely asking all the hard questions. She was facing what went wrong, especially her part in it. She stayed in the arena when it would have been very easy to leave all who knew her and land somewhere else where she could start over. Amy was not a rebellious, immoral woman, acting out an immoral life. She was a godly woman, left vulnerable and ignoring the protection of those who loved her, making frightened and exceedingly wrong choices.

. . . Awakening . . .

*All of us, left vulnerable by choosing to
ignore protection, are fully capable of
shocking and uncharacteristic wrong.*

. . . .

I was convinced of this about my daughter from the moment I received the news. It has never wavered.

….But still, I remained in shock.

Over the next months, I was emotionally and spiritually stuck. *How could this happen? I'm her father and her pastor. And somehow my own precious daughter chose to hide from us. Why did I not ask the right questions? Why didn't I see it? Why didn't I force my way in when I could see things weren't going well? How could I not know my own daughter was in distress, in a dark place?*

If our family has three values, one of them would be that we wouldn't need to hide. I think almost every day of their growing up I spoke these words to at least one of my kids:

"Did anything happen today that hurt your heart? Is anything scaring you? Is there anything you're not sure how to tell us? The only thing we can't protect you from is what we don't know."

Both Stacey and I have been pretty transparent about our failures, individually and together. If we had a fight, we made sure afterward to assure the children of our love and deep commitment. We told them what the argument was about and prayed God's protection for all of us. Because I had lived the destruction of playing a double life with my own parents, I asked God that such would never exist in my home.

Why did this way of life I preach not work for my own daughter when she most needed it? On top of that, I was devastated in believing that my family would no longer be able to represent this life in the way I thought we would.

How ridiculous! I was teaching grace everywhere, but I could not give the same grace now to myself. I did not yet understand the test of grace is not in keeping from failure, but in redeeming failure. Everyone will fail, under any view of God. How we treat each other when we do and how we find our lives again—this is where grace shines most brightly.

…It would take me quite a while to understand those words.

. . . Awakening . . .

I cannot protect my children in the subjectivity
of my shame but only in the objectivity of
trusting my God with me… and them.

, , , , , , , , , , ,

I began to experience the physiological symptoms of someone in shock. I developed this shaky, shuddering sensation in my shoulders and back. A chronic, anxious weakness, which left me sometimes unable to draw a full breath. My words came out clumsily, with too much effort. This condition would stay with me, undiagnosed, for the next two years.

I was still on the road in the following months, speaking often. But my shame was hissing at me that I wasn't fit to carry this message. Suddenly, I felt very much my age, and fifteen years more. I'd lost confidence. I wondered if I'd ever return to full strength. I was still trapped, months and months after that phone call. God would slowly have to untangle the lie I carried. The lie that said this should never have happened in a family that has believed these truths of grace so intentionally.

But He would show me that my understanding of grace does not make me or my children impervious to failure. No matter what I believe, each of my children has their own relationship with God, finding their own way, in their own choices. I do not have control over that.

. . . Awakening . . .

It's a mistake to make myself responsible for the choices of anyone else, even my own children.

, , , ... , , ,

This would be the last lie to be exposed.

Meanwhile, I was asking, "God, are You enough, now?" Some never get the freedom to risk asking it.

The third part of my life I spent trying to convince myself the

love I had found was enough.

I wrote this in the middle of my darkest hours…

Jesus, they say You were tempted in all ways, like other men. I know it's true. But You can't have experienced the particulars of my generational distortion and twisted understanding.

How can You enter in, tonight, with me, into this madness? I know You love me in all of it, that You enter fully into the pain of my suffering and grieving. I know You suffered more than I will ever understand. But can You really relate to the suffering of my failure and regret? Can You know what it feels like to be as torn up as me? How can a sinless God fully empathize with a human who still carries sin?

So I lie in bed tonight, afraid, alone, feeling unknown. It is irrationally flooding me, all at once; I've claimed trusting my identity solves much of this, but it has not been solved in me.

I am a bluffer who writes books on authenticity. I am sad my kids are at an age where they don't seem to need me as their pastor and protector. It makes me feel useless—like my best days are over. I fear my weakness makes me unattractive to my wife. I'm a controller. I use my fragility to avoid hard issues. I used to think I had the best friends in the world. Where are they now? What do I do that makes them leave? I lie about not wanting to be great. I spiritualize it into "having greater influence." I believe my issues would be solved if I was famous enough. I hate that I still carry that. I have held up my children as being nearly impervious to hiding. Now I feel foolish. I feel ashamed that my family now has a stigma attached to it. I get angry that I can't rally myself to again be the playful man of grace. I used to think my understanding of life made me immune to the regrets of life others carry. But tonight, regret is all I carry. Tonight, all of my demons are out. I have never felt so alone. Can You stand to be with me in this ugliness, or have I run You off also?

Then I remembered. And at least for that night, I was safe.

You became my sin. You drank every moment of it to the dregs. You bore my shame. Not only bore it, You have drawn closer to me, loved me more profoundly, and covered me even more in this mess, than ever before.

Tonight does not define me. It is real. I will experience it again. But I am never alone in it… Once again, I sigh and whisper out into the dark… "How did You find me here?"

And this:

So, the other night as we were drifting off to sleep, I asked, "Stacey, do you love me?" She answered, "Yes, I do. More than ever." I asked, "More than ever? Why?" She answered, "… Because you need me more than ever." And in the dark, I smiled, sighed, and fell fast asleep.

2012

ON THIS DAY I was flying to Indianapolis. I was returning to a conference where I'd had one of the most profound speaking experiences of my life four years before. That weekend, I had been on my game and sharp and funny and apparently profound.

I would speak tonight and the next night. I felt like crap. Whatever I had, it drew me inward and made me want to be left alone. I was tentative to talk much, because I couldn't get the words out as easily, in the short bursts this anxious constriction was allowing. I sounded confused, frail, and less intelligent.

I had mispacked for this conference. I'd been asked to dress "business casual." I didn't possess this particular look. I had "casual" and "slovenly" but not business casual. I had packed a pair of corduroys, but then discovered they were hopelessly wrinkled. I tried them on. I looked like I'd slept in them, several hundred times, on a rock quarry. I tried to iron them, but it made them look worse. Now they looked rumpled and starched. I had no choice. I walked out the door, looking like Rip Van Winkle heading out on a blind date.

Before the main session, I'd been asked to meet with a group who had been going through our book *The Cure*. I was not up to this. I could speak to a large group and bluff my way through, but in a small group, answering questions and such, I was a sitting duck. They'd see right through me.

I sighed, took a deep breath, and whispered to God, "Help me. I'm all cold and locked up. I don't want to fail. I don't want to let these people down. I don't want to let Trueface down. I don't want to let You down. I feel like I'm bluffing to be someone I used to be. I can't find myself right now. Help."

I walked into the room the group had reserved. Fifty or so were seated. I assumed they were waiting for me to say something insightful or wise. I had neither.

So I started talking, trying to teach something, about something. Until I was stopped, mid-bluff.

One of them stood and said these words: "John, we have something for you. For your board, your staff, and anyone else who has ever helped you stand in this gap until this original Good News found us. Would you give us the opportunity to each tell you how our lives are changed?"

For the next hour, one by one, they stood up and thanked God for us, telling their own personal stories of redemption. They were sobbing. Now I was sobbing. I was being given the gift of love from people I'd not previously known existed.

When they finished I stood up. "I did not want to come here tonight. I'm not doing well. I did not have anything much to give you." I gave them a five-minute version of the last year and a half.

Without a word spoken, they all walked up to me and put their hands on my shoulders. They prayed over me. That life-altering experience where you know you're not going through the motions, but actually believing God is present and powerful, doing something in that very moment. This meeting before the night's main session was a mightily important turning point for me.

John, I knew this hard and ugly time was going to hit you. So, I prepared this group to speak for Me tonight. I knew you would need it exactly now. Believe every word. I have been doing this through you behind the scenes. I thought tonight you should see a sample of it.

Don't think you have been disqualified or diminished because of what has happened this last year. No. This is your moment of validation. You are getting to test out if this way of life in grace holds when the unthinkable gets thought. Millions need to know you still believe it, teach it, and risk living it, even when you are shaky and without full breath.

Now, you're about to walk into the main session to speak. You look terrible. Your pants are wrinkled. You have a facial tic thing going. You will struggle to find your words. At several points, you'll get lost in your notes... For you have lost a step, or three. Fear not. In such weakness, if you let Me, I show up very strong. I've got this. All right, tie your shoe. I don't need you

falling off the stage...
  Be John Lynch. I'll be God. We work best this way.

2012

I WAS HOLDING the bread, taking communion that morning. I involuntarily asked myself, *Could I leave this? Could I do without this God, this faith, this life, all that has come to my soul with Jesus?* I was asking the horribly scary question I might have usually avoided, but now desperately needed to know my answer. Quickly, this came back: *Without Jesus, I can't make sense of anything. Forget heaven for a moment. Nothing today could hold my interest long, nothing could push back the absurdity and stop the emptiness if He is not real and near. Thirty years ago, there were so many other things I could have devoted myself to and fought valiantly for. I now have a life beyond anything I ever imagined. But without Jesus, none of it will hold me. He is the only meaning that gives value to every other relationship, and why I dare to get out of bed and face the horrible things I know may come to me.*

So I took the bread and then the cup. I not only had nowhere else to go, I could not face the rest of that day without His love, His life, His intimate knowledge of me, His risking to carry my name and give me His. I'll stay in His love... or I'll perish. Besides, He paid too much. It's not up for grabs.

2012

ON THIS DAY, sitting down to prepare a sermon, I instead found myself writing this:

John, I know you are not on your game these days. You have not been for some time now. I know you long with all your heart to be on your game. You have begged Me to get back to the clarity and strength of your past. I want you to know I probably will not be honoring that request. I do not say this with flippant indifference. This setback has given you a gift greater than you can yet know. You can hear. That's right. You're beginning to hear better. The pain, this lonely new longing, this shocking new shift inside you—it is waking up your heart. You are no longer feeling much in control. I hurt with you in the grief of what is no more. But I do not grieve over who you are maturing into. I do not need you to be on your game to have your life count magnificently. You will soon discover this is your most significant hour. I'm right here. I'm not playing you. This is not the result of your failure. By now, you must know better. I have taken the confusing loss this world has fashioned against you and I am turning it into the most significant hour of your life. You called to Me the other night in a way we'd never yet shared. It overwhelmed Me. Yes, Me. Would not the one who is fully love experience the fullest response to love? You are receiving My love these days. You are returning love. It is raw, unvarnished, and sputtering. But it is stunningly clear. Don't be afraid. You are not vanishing. You are not losing your mind. You are not losing your life. You are gaining it. I'm holding you together. This is what love ultimately longs to do. To be allowed to hold another together on this earth. Thank you, My friend.

2012

AT FIRST, *I wasn't sure. But yesterday I'm pretty certain I caught her glance as she was passing by. Noticing my eyes following her, she stopped and turned. We stared at each other, for nearly a minute. Then she smiled, as if in on a story and a series of events only she and I could fully appreciate. "Worry not, my friend. I'm not leaving. I'm circling back around for effect and a dramatic entrance. I'm here now. This current darkness is about to lift." I asked for her name. She said, "I wanted to be Joy, but it was already taken. My name is Hope." I involuntarily choked up as I barely got out these words: "I've missed you... more than you can know." She smiled again, kindly speaking directly into my eyes. "I doubt it. Now, cut the chit chat. I've got a dramatic entrance to make."*

Thank You, Father. Thank You for hearing my complaint, my honest pain and never imagining to hold it against me. Yesterday on the plane was the first time I've done that in years. This is all Your doing. I almost never complain to You. All along You've been waiting for me to get it out. It's what friends do. I'm sorry I've been pretending like I wasn't disappointed. I was. You knew. You know me perfectly. And You knew it was all part of this particular ride. You are more stunning and real than I have ever known. Please keep renewing my heart. I am worth little to others without my passion and playful hope. Oh, she stopped and talked to me yesterday.

Hope. You caused that. Thank You, my stunning God. Thank You.

Love, John

2013

MY WIFE AND I were sitting by the fireplace that night. We sat out there a lot. Our children were no longer in our home. Carly was studying at Azusa Pacific University. Caleb and Amy both lived nearby, here in Phoenix. Caleb and his wife Kali now had two children of their own. We had family dinners every Monday evening on this patio.

This evening, it was just us two. And a kale salad. She makes a killer kale salad! Black kale with lots of fresh garlic and lemon. You wish you knew someone who could make this salad.

Strands of lights hung above us. I was taking in this entire patio. All of it—this entire adobe and cobalt-tiled center, with fireplace, barbecue, and gas lamp—was a surprise and a gift. Ten years before, some of our best friends built all this on the weekend we were away for my fiftieth birthday. It has been the backdrop for so many of our celebrations, graduations, and best times with family and friends.

Forks were scraping plates, while the crackle of cheap alley wood played in the background. I love this particular combination of sounds.

I sighed.

It was a noticeably different sigh that night. Wonderfully different from the sighs of the past two years. It was the sigh of contentment. *God. You've done it. You've been God to this family. You are protecting us. You are redeeming this chaos. We're still intact.*

Over the last year, Stacey and I were enjoying our marriage like never before.

. . . *Awakening* . . .

When crisis hits long and hard enough, we are forced to decide whether we will blame each other or, instead, more deeply need each other.

, , ... , . .

By the absolute grace of God, we had learned to need each other more deeply. Stacey was recuperating from uterine cancer surgery. The cancer turned out to be relatively noninvasive. But there is nothing routine about the time between being told something is very wrong and hearing the diagnosis. And there is nothing noninvasive about the robotic surgery which removed her uterus. But she faced it with such serenity, dignity, and trust in God. It made her even more attractive and beautiful to my very soul. I'm in such awe of my wife. She has faced so much and yet is more mature, fun, and safe than ever before. She allowed me to be strong for her.

She also learned to allow me to be needy. In the past, she had resented anything needy about me. No more. She embraced my need. She's not afraid of my frailness. She has become my safest place. And something about her protection was making me more confident and strong.

God saw this coming all along. I had always loved Stacey. But there were times when I wanted to slip off to Burma and sell pamphlets on a street corner. I suspect there have been times where she wanted to club me in my sleep, wrap me up in carpet, tie it off with duct tape, drive me into the desert, and leave me for dead.

This love, I think, was born of dependence. I'm not sure I had always allowed my heart to need her. I'm not sure I knew how to let her in to protect me. She absolutely altered her life and dreams once she knew I needed her.

She glanced over at me, noticing my sigh. She could tell it was different. After twenty-nine years she could tell a change in sighs. It was quiet for a while. She was trying to gather the words which had been forming for some time. Sitting together under the same blanket, both of us staring into the fire, she said,

"You don't see it, do you? You are the last to see the magic He is accomplishing in you."

"What do you mean?"

"I love you so much, John Lynch. You don't see who you are, do you? You don't see what God's revealing. You are missing what has been taking place in you. You've been all bummed out, like it will always be hard. You can't see what we all see. So, let me tell you what I see. This last year has revealed you in magnificence, my husband. You are more kind to me. You don't power up. You don't make me feel judged. At least not as often. You're listening to my heart. You're more tender towards God. I am more at peace because of it. You are less opinionated, with fewer critiques you'll go to the wall for. God has done all this while you thought you were only holding on. I would never have thought I'd thank Him for this last hurricane season of sadness. But tonight, with all my heart, I do."

I sighed again.

. . . Awakening . . .

*It's not only how God sees me on my worst day,
but what He does in me through my worst day
that reveals the true nature of Christ in me.*

. . . .

It happened. It was happening this evening. It would mark me for the rest of this ride. **This fourth part of my life I am actually beginning to experience the life love has given me.**

2013

FORGIVE ME. I am a list writer. I could not adequately express in a story, what God taught me in my period of great darkness... my worst day. All of these, I imagine, could be considered "Awakenings." Thank you for indulging me.

. . . *Awakening* . . .

For faith to avail, it usually must first
appear as though it might not.

.　.　.　.　.　.　.　.　.　.　.

- Christ's love holds even more fiercely in the storm.
- A tested grace is superior to an idealized grace.
- Fragile but authentic trust is more enjoyable to God than strong inborn capacity.
- I let go of some expectations of God while forming new and more significant ones.
- Love is experienced most when it is needed most.
- The best life is not the one with the least pain or suffering.
- God goes on doing His beauty when I opt out of trusting Him. It's just that I miss it.
- The enjoyment of friends is more sacred when I rediscover them in my need.
- Jesus does not change in my darkest times. He remains a playful and true romantic.
- Jesus is enough… and He cannot and will not ever be taken from me.
- Laughter in a hard season is like stumbling upon a great red wine in a bus-stop cafeteria.

2013

DURING THESE DAYS my life was marked by one singular block directly outside my home. The place where God met me—where I most accurately reflected on where I'd been and where I was going—was no longer in a pulpit, on the road, or in words typed onto an electronic page. Every time her parents brought her over, my nearly two-year-old granddaughter Maci pointed to the front door and urgently pleaded these words to me: "Alk. Bawi. Apa." I chose to believe she was saying, "Walk. Bali. Pops." Bali was my dog. Pops is me. The walk was the two-hundred-yard stretch down to the corner and back. I used to carry her. She now loved walking nearly the entire route. I used to run four hundred yards in fifty seconds. It now took the three of us over twenty minutes. They were the most sacred minutes of my week. Shuffling along, looking at details of a journey I had rarely before noticed. This was all new to me. I'd been slowly learning for it to be enough. On this stretch, I was Maci's safety net, allowing her to explore her new world. She was becoming my safety net to reexamine this world I'd stopped exploring a while back. I'd kiss her and tell her I love her. She whispered back with a tender, trusting smile, "Yeah." In that moment, moments just past sunset, I shuffled along, with two creatures who thought I was one of the greatest humans alive, God surrounded the event. I'm almost sure He was saying,

I have not forgotten. Someday, you will shuffle this walk with someone taking your hand. Today, we are walking this walk, because holding her hand is healing you. All, so you can go back out and run, in health. Take your time. I'm in no hurry. I know what's up ahead. 'Tis all grace, My friend. Now, stop daydreaming. She's out in the street again. You might not want to let her put that cat poop in her mouth.

I looked back. She was wearing a diaper and no shoes. We must've been a sight to anyone passing by—a senile old man mindlessly wandering ahead of a child he could no longer find or dress. I scooped her up and carried her for a bit. In that moment, I was the happiest I'd been in a very long time.

2013

THERE WERE DAYS when I wanted to say, "Okay, Judiazers, you win. Live in your damned duplicity and corrupted sham! Poison the next generation, and the next. Knock yourselves out." I had tried to walk away and show up somewhere to preach polite messages the majority would enjoy. But it was like convincing myself to give up my love for Cockburn's music in favor of *The Greatest Hits of Carrot Top*.

Again, here I go with the lists. But I thought you must see some of the tenets which have informed and animated my life. This way of life is starting to happen more and more. But the loudest voice out there is still missing it. In this list, I give the hope of unbridled grace and shed light on the damage that can be caused when that same grace is not unleashed.

I dream in color of the Church one day:

- drawing out each other's new natures, instead of comparing behaviors.
- moving closer to each other when we fail.
- gaining permission to protect each other.
- creating environments of grace where there is safety to not hide.
- enjoying the intimate and unguarded closeness of a God who is already pleased with us.
- reaching to others with a Gospel of hope for today, not only a remedy for heaven.
- living with heartfelt obedience instead of religious compliance.
- giving our lives away as a response of love not as an effort to assuage our shame.
- breaking the "ought code" that is anesthetizing our kids from intimacy with Jesus.
- taking the moralistic filter off of God's Word, so it no longer condemns us.
- believing we're adored on our worst day, so we are free to take off the mask.
- resting in the absolute reality that a shame-free story has been purchased for us.

Until that shift, our churches will continue to:

- try to change people who are already completely changed.

- measure our righteousness by how little we sin.
- withhold love from others because we're too busy earning love.
- believe knowing what is right is the same as the power to do right.
- be goaded to figure out how to please God, when He is already fully pleased.
- fail to protect each other, afraid, behind our fears of rejection.
- equate masculinity with machismo, thinking this will break our passivity.
- create more systems, techniques, programs, and methodology, thinking it will give us Jesus.
- beat ourselves up thinking, somehow, we will finally arrive at being enough.
- convince ourselves He is out there, over there, and up there instead of in here.
- not believe we are righteous, but instead live like saved, disappointing sinners.
- still think the correct slogan is "It's not about me." How ridiculous. It's about Him in us.

Soon, very soon, John. This is the Church I dream of too and can see on the horizon. It may not be you who gets to see this, but it will happen before I return. This is My message. It is My responsibility. Your part is to keep trying new ways to get behind the lines.

2013

LATE ONE AFTERNOON, Stacey and I opened a bottle of wine to sit out front and watch the sky change colors. The back of the bottle bore this description: "This blend presents aromas of fresh mixed red berries, juicy cherries, and hints of vanilla… that linger with red fruit notes through a long, smooth finish. Enjoy this wine with salads, pasta, and meats."

If there were any truth in advertising the label would read: "This bottle of swill is harsh and undesirable at first and then subtly changes into what kelp, vinegar, resin, and burlap might taste like if allowed to age between the nubs of a moldy shower mat. Enjoy this wine with food that starts with the letter x."

2013

NADINE HOUSTON AND my wife pulled a masterful surprise on their husbands. Doug and I discovered on the way to our respective airports that we were going to meet together in Las Vegas.

The Houston and Lynch families had become lifelong friends these last few years. Doug and Nadine had been wonderfully transformed by these truths of grace since hearing a recording of a talk I gave years before called "The Two Roads." Doug had recently been working incredibly hard, under intense pressure, in his businesses. The women decided what he needed most was to wander around Las Vegas.

With me! Sweet mother of creamed corn!

For three days, the four of us dined at some world-class restaurants. We bought really cool shoes at a store Stacey and I normally only walked past on dates. Doug and I were treated to an hour-long shaving experience, wearing hot face towels scented with something smelling like lemon cream pie. The four of us strolled the Strip and spent an entire evening at a prestigious steak house overlooking the Bellagio water show. We drank Scotch that famous generals never got to taste. We stayed up late and then slept in as long as we wanted, in fancy hotel rooms with those heavy, pitch-black curtains, electronically closing on their own. We were playing like dressed-up kids, driving a showroom Mustang convertible, cruising down Main Street on a warm Saturday night.

Nadine had also booked us to see a Garth Brooks concert.

I'm not a huge country western fan, but she had heard he put on a fantastic show. If they wanted to see Garth Brooks, then so did we.

Just minutes before the show began Nadine and Doug had to leave. Nadine is allergic to crab. She had eaten some at dinner, disguised as langostino, less than an hour before. We were deeply sad for them, and a little sad for us. Stacey and I were now sitting next to each other at a concert we might not have ever chosen.

What followed was one of my favorite three-hour blocks of time I've had in my life.

There was no band, no pyrotechnics. It was Garth, a single spotlight, and his guitar, in a relatively small room. He had put together an evening to honor all of the musical influences who had helped form his music. He was brilliant, winsome, anecdotal, funny, heart-breaking, heartwarming, and deeply inspiring. For three hours he kept a beer-drinking audience spellbound with black hats and boots, who were expecting a night of rowdy country-western. Instead, they were getting artistry and life and hope. Cynical, intellectual hipsters would've been deeply moved. We were watching the culmination of a man's journey. He was brilliantly and naturally walking us through the life-shaping moments that came from hearing songs in his room on transistor radios and the radio dial of his father's car. After each song, he bowed and gave the name of the artist he'd been lauding. It was profound, nostalgic, and immensely entertaining. We were riveted in our chairs. He was walking us through our own experience of the last decades. He was helping us interpret our own timelines. It is hard to say these words, but that evening may have been one of the finest shows I've ever seen.

But much, much more was happening for me that evening. As we slowly moved with the crowd leaving the theater, my wife turned to me.

"I only know of two people in the world who have that kind of passion and storytelling ability to pull off such an evening. I'm standing next to one of them. John, forgive me for the times I have devalued your gift, and not supported it, or helped to promote it out of you so you could give it to others."

I was dazed. We shuffled along with the exiting crowd, in silence. I was smiling, rocked by my wife's intimate knowledge of who I longed to be at my core.

God spoke to my heart in the moment.

Don't miss this, John. I arranged for you to see this tonight.

Worry not for Doug and Nadine. They will be cheering what I did for you. Besides, I am soon taking them on a cruise with their family that will cause them to momentarily forget your name. We are far from done with this journey. You are healing, maturing, coming alive, becoming free. You no longer carry the heavy bags that kept you from giving your version of the evening you just watched. You saw your future this evening. Listen to Stacey. Dream big, My friend. Dream with your heroes. Tell them what I'm telling you. They will know what to do with it. Tell them you're ready. Tell them you're not afraid. Then tell them you're very afraid. Tell them you're fully alive. Tell them you still have one long ride left in you. I have so many to reach, whose hearts will be opened only by story and self-effacing humor. What you learned in a VW doing all-night talk shows; what you learned on the stage for Dr. Witt; what you have learned telling stories in messages, I am now going to release. I've been doing it all along, but this may actually become your finest hour. Go figure.

Well, that's all I can tell you right now. This whole thing is still run by trust, not pre-information.

Kid, this is some of the payoff of your worst days. I never stop working in you. I never stop seeing the big picture. I never stop protecting what I put on your heart all those years ago. Sleep well, My friend. You're going to need it.

2013

I WAS LISTENING to "The Good America" by Keith Jarrett one evening, sitting outside on the patio with my dog. I had my earbuds in. Stacey was at a baby shower. Inside, thieves could have been rifling through our refrigerator, filling their satchels with yogurt and cilantro. Out on the patio, life was very, very good. *Pillage away thieves, pillage away. Just don't come out to the patio and disturb me. My wallet is on the dresser. Leave me alone to my evening with my God...*

Summer, 2013

WE WERE IN Puerto Penasco, Mexico. "We" was my entire family—myself, Stacey, Caleb, Kali, Amy, Carly, and our grandchildren, Maci and Payton. We were on vacation.

Amy and I were on the beach... running.

That last phrase may mean little to you. To me, it carries more unbridled splendor than I have keystrokes to convey.

First, I was sixty. I had not "run" in over a decade. Yes, I'd limped the old-man-survival-shuffle for blocks at a time. It was more of an extended, controlled fall than a jog.

I ran a marathon once. Back when people could still watch a movie outdoors. From their car.

I'd damaged my legs badly back in the early '90s. I had tried to run several miles back home one day on a badly strained calf. I was never the same since. I had gone to a specialist about it, unwilling to give up running. He did a few tests and took some internal pictures. He deadpanned these words: "John, when you think of your calf muscles, imagine strands of beef jerky, loosely tied to a bone on either end."

Nice bedside manner, Doc.

But God had formed today's scene, from long before oceans and sand existed. We started out so slowly. I predicted my shuffle would be stopped by muscle tightness and shooting pain, as it usually did. But something about this setting, out on firm sand, with an ocean to my right and my daughter on my left, was different than usual.

There was no pain. There was no limp. With each step, there was less caution.

I gradually picked up the pace. Amy and I were now breathing in unison, striding down the shore. I took off my shirt. I felt almost thirty-three again!

I became quickly aware this was no longer a run. It was the revealing of God's vindicating and redemptive love and eternal intention.

I continued to stride out, faster and faster. "Faster" might've been a nine-minute pace. But I had not felt this familiar feeling of well-earned exertion in so long! It was normally very painful. Except I'd missed it so much, I was gulping it all in, with every breath.

Nearly two miles into the run, Amy looked over at me. She stared a long time. I could feel her gaze. I looked back over at her. We were both beaming at each other, now nearly galloping.

I turned back, straight ahead, pushing forward even faster. She called out, above the sound of the waves, this one word: "Impressive."

We were locked into a moment of God's finest quality of appreciation. I was lost in the eternal, lost in how absolutely great He is.

I was lost in my love for my daughter, lost in my respect, admiration, and endless pride of who she is—maturing into a far more beautiful woman than the one I knew before the darkness. She was healing, coming fully alive, fully herself, deeply in love with God.

She was opening again to me. It felt like that day when I opened her car door to discover all those note cards taped to her dash. Later that evening, she and I would opt out of the family trip into town. We would dress up and go on a date, strolling around this resort. We would continue to allow each other back into the deep places of trust and love.

I mouthed this word back to her, with insufficient breath to make it audible: "Impressive."

I was lost in shattered gratitude.

As my body began to seize up into near crisis, I was unwilling to allow this moment to end. God was revealing Himself again, in such intensity, I momentarily wondered if I would suddenly have a heart attack and come home. He has been more to me than I ever imagined I had capacity to experience. I was ready. I pushed harder, happily forcing the issue for God.

And I said this word to Him inside my head, breathing now in short gasps: *Impressive.*

On My Worst Day

It Continues...

...SO, WE HAVE arrived at the point where *On My Worst Day* originally ended. Personally, I thought it was a pretty strong closing chapter. But, in 2020, Trueface kindly gave John Lynch Speaks the rights to the book. And at a meeting I attended, on a cold winter's day in Canada, the idea came to someone, "Hey, why don't we bring the book up to the present day?" Everyone in the room smiled and nodded.

Someone (it may have been me) once said, "The most important time in your life is now, until it's not." Most of us discover some of our most important stories are yet to come. At the same time, God is always, quietly and often unnoticed, forming and shaping our worst days into our best days. In this new section, some of my early worst-day stories have found beautiful resolution. I still shake my head at how God does that for each of us.

I am so excited and humbled for you to turn the pages on the rest of these stories. I'm praying, as you read them that you will, even more deeply, experience your journey with Jesus into this grace. And maybe you too will witness God beautifully resolve some worst days into best ones.

On My Worst Day

Fall
2013

MY RUN ON the Puerto Peñasco beach in Mexico with my daughter Amy seems like two lifetimes ago. By 2013, my body had become full of pain. I could have endured it better if only I'd known what was causing it, or if the quickly developing debilitations I was experiencing would end up taking my life. *Was there something I could've or should've been figuring out about what was happening inside of me? Why would symptoms I thought were gone forever, suddenly seem to return out of nowhere? What do I say to those who keep telling me that I look just fine?* I had no idea how I was going to keep speaking at events when I couldn't even concentrate. And I feared that I might never recapture my sense of humor or confidence...

My calendar had become predominantly filled with lumbar punctures, EKGs, EMGs, MRIs, nerve conduction studies, and biopsies. One day, I was given an EKG to try to determine the source of new daily intermittent twitching. The older man administering the test disinterestedly mumbled, "You don't have ALS. But you do have neuropathy." Neuro-what?! What's neuropathy? He explained it had to do with damaged nerve endings.

There are four main types of neuropathy. The large fiber neuropathy form eventually takes your feeling sensors away from you. The small fiber form causes increasingly intense burning, like running barefoot across asphalt, in the summer, over and over. I was diagnosed with *that* one. At that moment, my new reality was that neuropathy would now compete for my attention at every event I would speak at, and in every conversation I would have, in every relationship, for the foreseeable future.

I was prayed over almost everywhere I went. I cherished it. But some seemed clearly disappointed when their prayers didn't immediately heal me. Like I was doing something wrong. I wanted to say, "Look champ, I didn't ask you to pray for me. I really do believe God can heal me. I want your prayers to work—much more than you! But I'm in way too much pain to carry the added pain of disappointing you." Sometimes I would try to pretend that I wasn't feeling as much pain as I was just to make others feel that their prayers had been successful. They were looking for complete healing from my head to my toes. The least I could do was report back a 2 percent improvement.

Everywhere I spoke, wonderfully intentioned friends gave me books and website links about Lyme disease, healing mats, elixirs, balms, essential oils, special socks, and the benefits of walking barefoot on natural surfaces. Neurologists began moving from talk of a cure to pain management. Pain was making a coward out of me. I felt exceedingly alone in that chronic pain. I hate the word chronic.

I imagine Jesus saying,

John, you tell others you trust My sovereignty. I know you do. But there is a barely discernible line between claiming you're at peace because you trust My sovereignty, and stuffing your pain down trying to protect Me from looking bad. John, I don't need you to defend My reputation. Stacey and I both wish you would just allow yourself to cry, to scream, and to tell Me what you're really thinking and feeling. I can handle unkind words formed from pain. This is an honest and accurate response to what you're going through. I'm not offended by the language of pain. I know your heart. Faith does not demand stoic fatalism.

Kid, there will be no cure for what you have. There is nothing you will discover with enough online reading. This condition traces to the Fall. Every human body has death in it, manifested in a million, unique expressions. I have already stopped and prevented endless damage and destruction in you. You'll see this only when you get home. For now, let Me hold you. Learn to walk with Me in this unraveling time. It will not take the pain away, but it will, at times, transcend the pain. Goodnight, My son. You are not falling behind the parade, though it feels like it. So, sleep. I will be restoring your soul for tomorrow, while you dream of feeding pelicans, with Jim Gaffigan's aunt, waist-deep in a fountain, outside a casino. I'm pretty sure there's nothing to figure out in this dream. But I do like Gaffigan.

On My Worst Day

2014

I WAS ON my morning walk. My health was going downhill so quickly. My neuropathy was getting more painful by the day, and there was no silver bullet to stop it. I developed an upper-body shuddering—I have no other way to describe it. It pulled me in on myself. I felt shaky and small. I couldn't get a grip or a full breath. I was operating at about forty percent. And that forty percent was highly suspect. I became afraid of going on the road, fearing that others would be able to see it.

I generally operate with a high view of God's sovereignty. How can you argue cogently with a Being who is never wrong; ethically or logically? So, I generally accept what comes. I may whine to Stacey, but I don't question God much. But I never imagined my health deteriorating like this in the prime of my life. He is fully good and will make no mistakes regarding me, but I needed to know if I could handle the suffering coming up. So, this one particular morning I decided to ask some questions, ones I don't think I'd ever asked.

All my life my only calling card has been my communication abilities. What will happen if I can no longer use my gifts? Who will I become? Will my life still be meaningful? God, please find a way to speak to me. Would You give me a sign, please? I am so lost.

I didn't usually ask God for signs. He knows how to find me. But I was full-on desperate. I was begging the God of the universe for a sign to show me that He had heard me and that everything was going to be alright. I continued to call out to Him, *Please, show me today that You've heard me.*

I walked outside and sat down in a chair on the patio. I've spoken with God many times there. If He was going to give me a sign this might be where He'd do it.

Suddenly, out of seemingly nowhere, there were birds chirping to me. Three of them, perched on a strand of lights, less than four feet in front of me. They were chirping like they were urgently trying to communicate with me. They were so loud.

Wait. Was this it? Was God meeting with me? Not knowing what else to do, I started talking to them. "Hey, little guys. I'm John Lynch. I think we've seen each other before. Thank you for meeting with me. So… Well then... You're sure loud for such little birds."

I wondered, *God, is this You speaking to me through these birds? Thank You. But how do I make out what You're saying through them? Am I missing something? I'm not leaving this spot until I understand what You're saying to me through them.*

Minutes of this banter continued. Then it dawned on me. I was directly between those birds and a weathered hole in the eaves; which had become a nursery for baby cactus wrens. This hole was directly behind me. These angry parents had baby wrens they were trying to get to. They weren't talking to me. They were yelling at me.

Oh, well. So much for my Pentecostal encounter with God speaking to me through birds. I questioned what I was doing. God had never interacted with me like that before. I had to get a grip and face reality with acceptant faith. I felt a little foolish. I went inside, showered, got dressed, and got on with whatever it is I did with my days. Several hours later, I grabbed my keys and wallet, and headed for the door.

The moment I turned to close the front door he was there. Immediate. Fixed. Stationary. Maybe fifteen inches from my face. A hummingbird. For whatever reason, I didn't flinch or swing wildly. That hummingbird did not move. Neither of us were moving, or blinking, or glancing away. There we were. Two of God's creatures transfixed on each other. This hummingbird had been sent. Ten seconds, twenty seconds, thirty seconds. Wow! What was happening? That half a minute in front of a whirring hummingbird seemed like five minutes. I found myself imagining what this hummingbird might be trying to communicate to me. I imagined his voice quavering:

"Hey, so, listen. Um, I don't generally do this. This is really scary. But, I've been sent to you, of all the creatures in the universe, to represent your God. He heard your request today. And, oh, what am I doing? I think I might pass out! Anyway, He has sent me to you. He reasoned that if I stay fixed in front of you, maybe you'd know something big is going on. He wants you to know He loves you. And that He's got you. He's been up ahead. This turns out really well. Ok? Um, there might have been more, but I have to get out of here."

With those final words, in a blink, he was gone.

I waited to see if he would circle back around. But the moment had passed.

You might be thinking, *Well, John has quite an imagination.* And, that I do have. But the real trick there was that God found a way to speak to me through a creature who couldn't speak. My Creator caused me to imagine exactly what He knew I needed to hear from Him. He caused me to hear it through a hummingbird so that I would never forget it. Now, that's cool. And supernatural.

At the end of the day, what an honor it must have been for that little guy to represent all of creation in getting a message from God to a human. What a story he had to tell! Most hummingbirds don't get to do something like that in their three to five-year lifespan.

It is enough to say that I have never asked for another sign. That one got through just fine. Well played, my brave hummingbird friend. Well played.

November, 2014

I DID NOT see this one coming.

Nadine and Doug Houston and one of their daughters, Lauren, planned a trip for the three authors of *The Cure*, and their families— the Lynchs, the Thralls, and the McNicols—to visit the Holy Land.

Trying to recap a trip to Istanbul, Ephesus, Jordan, the Sea of Galilee, the Dead Sea, Jerusalem, and Bethlehem in a few paragraphs is like doing a thirty-second infomercial on God's love.

All of it was, and still is, astonishing. But there was one moment that was transformative above all the others. But it sure didn't start out that way.

Our guide on one particular day had just mumbled an itinerary to us from the front of the bus. He had a thick accent and I missed most of it. We had already observed so much. Today, I wasn't really in the moment. It was an uncommonly muggy, hot day. We were in a low-lying, dusty area. We stopped at a restroom in what seemed like the middle of nowhere. Bugs were everywhere. And let me tell you, flies in the Holy Land are no less offensive than the ones in my backyard. I wanted nothing more than to be back at our nice hotel.

My anticipation to witness the next "possible site of religious importance" was growing less enthusiastic by the tour. Guide after guide had said it in similar ways about various sites: "My friends, right here is *possibly* where Jesus made the fire for Peter when he swam to shore that morning… Or, it *might* have been on the other side of the lake. No one knows for sure. Enjoy."

We stepped out of our air-conditioned, elegant vehicle onto more dusty, dry terrain. Geesh! I could get hot dust back in Phoenix. I was spacing out, in a funk, when I noticed it was becoming increasingly green in front of us. I walked a few more steps and heard what sounded like running water. Then, like coming out of a stupor straight into a vision, I saw hills nearby to my right. They were riddled with caves. In a moment, I knew where I was. I was at the Jordan River. Somewhere very, very close to where John baptized Jesus!

And. I. Was. Undone.

I immediately took off my shoes and socks and placed my hands and feet into the water. I was sobbing.

I had always declared that there was no place more God-infused than another—I could experience Him mightily in a mall parking lot and miss His presence at a mountain-top cathedral. But suddenly, a story I'd read was becoming my personal experience.

All I could think was, *Jesus, I feel so bad. The other day when I toured the site where they said You were crucified, it was so covered in the trappings of religious adoration and centuries of gaudy trinkets, I couldn't sense You there. I was disconnected, alone, disappointed. I felt like there must have been something wrong with me that the most important place of Christian faith could feel so cold to me, while everyone around me seemed so moved. But here, here at the Jordan*

River, I feel You as close as at any time in these last thirty-five years. I don't want to leave here.

Scenes from throughout my life began to quickly flash in front of me. The boy in the flannel uniform at the Little League field, the boxcar, the night running through the streets in the rain when Arlene broke up with me. On and on, memories flooded me. Seminary, Stacey... Then, suddenly, my kids flashed into my thoughts.

Jesus, what would have become of me, if You didn't come here to this very spot to meet up with John the Baptist? No Caleb, no Amy, no Carly. You allowed faith to enter into my family line. You kept me from the self-protected, crippled destiny I was forming. I was a faker with a heart that couldn't make sense of my life. I was less trusting, more wounded, more hidden, more full of shame, and self-protecting cynicism. I had no source of love. The power of His healing, the staggering strength of what it feels like to experience His presence and delight washed over me. *Oh, my Jesus, I am out of words. Let this water invade my pores. I never want to forget.*

Stacey soon walked up behind me and draped her arms over my shoulders. She kissed my head. And we stood together, crying. I told her what was happening inside of me and what I'd been seeing and discovered God had been showing her the power of what He had done in her life as well.

Up until that very moment, I had never felt fully at home in my faith. It was as if I had somehow slipped in through a clerical error. Sure, I knew that despite any failures He loved and accepted us all, but somehow, my failures were different. They were pathetic, almost egocentrically narcissistic. And regardless of what I "knew," I just couldn't shake the belief that "my type" shouldn't get Jesus. Shame told me I didn't fit with those He loved. Like a deranged murderer who gets invited by a generous host to a dinner party—the other guests are simply forced to take you in—but you stand out; untrusted, unwanted. You're in, but you don't have the pedigree. For me, it was as if I could never fully get the dope resin off my fingers, and no amount of seminary or pastoring could fully convince me otherwise. But there at the Jordan River, in that very moment, I knew that no one else in all of history may belong, but I belonged. I cupped my hands and tried to hold the holy water to my face.

I belong. I belong. I belong.

Eventually, I allowed us to leave the river. We got back on the bus and headed back to our hotel. I was silent most of the evening. I think I feared if I talked too much, I'd lose my new sight.

Even my new heart hasn't stopped me from learning to gradually "normalize" my faith in God. My new birth has been melded with swim meets, pastoral expectations, and home repairs. The chronic pain I experience and the unanswered prayer have unwittingly taught me to moderate my adoration of God. But there, at the shore of the Jordan River, there, half a world away from my normal, it was back. The God I originally came for. No, wait... a God better than I came for. I wasn't a new believer—but I felt like one—I was a mature believer, with several jolts of nitroglycerine.

I got up the next day and visited the next site that changed history. And then the next. Then I boarded a plane and returned to the zip code where I live out my faith daily.

Except that moment at the Jordan River happened. And no one can take it from me. That moment in time will protect me and guide me for the rest of my journey. I never saw it coming.

Thank you, Jesus of Nazareth. Jesus of the Jordan. Jesus of my belonging.

On My Worst Day

2015

SHE BURST THROUGH the door carrying half a dozen bags. She flashed that understated, confident, half-smile that only Stacey can make. Without any words at all, that smile is able to magically articulate this very thought: *Wait 'til you see what I just got you at the store. Oh, my gosh! You're going to be so thankful you married me.*

I smiled back. "So, what did you get me?"

"How do you know I got you anything?"

"Your smile."

"Give me a second," she said as she made her way to the bedroom. She called back, "You're going to be so thankful you married me." Seconds later she called out, "Ok, you can come in now."

Carefully laid out on my side of the bed was a shirt. She has purchased hundreds of them for me over these years. Often she leaves them in the bag for me to pull out, explaining that she can easily take them back if I don't like them. Occasionally though, she knows she's nailed it. Those pieces of clothing she spreads neatly out on our bed. This particular one she'd brought home was a short-sleeved white shirt. It had blue marlins on it. I did like it. It looked really cool.

"So...?" she questioned.

Apparently, my nod wasn't sufficient. "Yes. I like it, a lot. Thanks for getting this. You know I'm always looking for a short-sleeved dress shirt that doesn't make me look nerdy."

She looked at me, then at the shirt, then back at me. I looked one more time. Then it hit me as I made the nostalgic connection. The fish shirt!

I breathed deeply several times before I could respond. "Oh my gosh, Stacey! You, you did it. I'd forgotten all about it." I ran the several steps to her and held her.

"No. You didn't forget. You told me the fish shirt story as recently as this month. All your children can repeat it."

I was maybe seven. My dad and I were in the den. I was fixated on the cool shirt he was wearing. Side note: for several years I'd sort of believed my dad was Superman. He, for his family's protection, of course, had kept it secret from my brother and me, as he has for the rest of mankind.

Everything my dad wore was cool. But this shirt. Dang. The following conversation ensued.

"Dad, I really like your shirt."

"This shirt? With the fish on it?"

"Yes."

"You really like it, huh?"

"I really do."

"Then I'll get you one just like it!"

"You will?"

"Yes. Then, we'll have the same shirt."

"Wow, dad. Thanks."

Weeks went by. No shirt. Months went by. No shirt. Years went by. No shirt.

I don't know if my dad couldn't find it and got embarrassed, or if he forgot. But I did not forget. I told myself that he must have been working really hard to find it. That the shirt must have been very expensive. Or rare. I knew he'd find it though and that one day he'd walk through the door with that shirt.

My dad passed away at eighty-six. It's not like he didn't have enough time to find it. If he had just mentioned it to Mom she would have found one, wrapped it, and made it look like he had brought it home himself, just for me. She wanted him to be my hero—moms do that.

Dads should not forget the promises they make to their kids. Especially when their son actually thinks they're Superman! There's only a short window of time when kids believe their dads can do anything. For me, I couldn't help but wonder how my dad could fly in and save people from a burning building, yet couldn't find me a fish shirt. I would have been fine if he'd brought home a white shirt and then drawn a fish on it with a felt pen. For decades, I've told this story without it having a good ending. Many fathers and sons keep living stories without good endings. I'm not the first son who was still waiting for something from his dad.

Enter Stacey into my life. She does not forget such things. She catalogs each one of them in her heart. Then she waits for the perfect moment. If I could do what Stacey does, you'd have your shirt by this afternoon. I have no tolerance for perfect timing or patience. Stacey can wait entire years for the right moment to come along—for the perfect time to give the perfect gift. For years, she would casually ask me what kind of fish were on dad's shirt. We'd be sitting on a beach somewhere and out of nowhere, she'd say, "You remember that shirt your dad had with all the fish on it? I've always wondered what color it was." She was collecting data. Then she would wait. And remember.

In the end, this ultimately isn't a story of what my dad didn't do. It's the glorious story of what my precious wife does. Used of God, she helps redeem some of my broken stories. Where would I be without the gift of her in my life? Where would I be if I had to tough it out, with only those around me who admired, but didn't love me? If love is the process of meeting needs, and it is, then few know love better than my girl. Stacey knew that having that shirt was more than a wish for me. It had become a need. As of the time this book was published, my fish shirt is six years old. I wear it once, sometimes twice a week, in the spring, summer, and even into the early fall. To avoid the wear and tear of washing it, I simply put it back on the hanger several wears at a time—it means too much to me to risk it in the dirty clothes pile.

Recently, at a friend's birthday party, a woman I'd never before met, walked up to me at the kitchen island taco bar. She touched my shoulder and gushed, "This is the nicest shirt! It's so crisp and white. And I love those fish. Did someone get this shirt for you?" I thought, *Oh ma'am. You have no idea. Do you see that woman across the room? The one with the blond hair and that confident half-smile? That's my wife. She loves me. She got me this shirt. Let's just say my dad had one a long time ago. I'm not certain he wasn't Superman...*

2015

I LONG FOR the next generation of Christ-followers to lose their fear of an unbridled grace. Grace does not need to be balanced with anything. Love does not need to be mitigated by anything. This grace alone can set our new nature free to live in heartfelt obedience and playful joy. The Scriptures are wonderfully full of all manner of things to do and obey. But it's all about how we accomplish them. A man-made system will create obligatory compliance; grace will create heartfelt obedience. There is power in grace. No man-made manipulation, coercion, or raised eyebrows of the moralist will do much of anything. Please risk for this grace. For the sake of your children and a watching world, wanting to believe in Jesus. They call us hypocrites because they watch us lecture on the sins we don't struggle with and hide the sins we do. Instead, grace allows us to depend upon Christ in us while faking nothing in the meantime. It's a beautiful way to live. You get to smile a lot.

Grace is not meant to free us from obeying the heart of God. Grace is the nutrient-rich soil that seeds of truth drop into so they're not choked out by the self-condemnation of failure. Instead, no longer afraid of God's disgust, we can obey God from the heart rather than from compliance. And we grow into a beautiful, healthy tree that gives shade to others.

2015

I DISCOVERED IN 2015 that I was speaking more and more to people who were ready to admit that they were fragile and failed. And while we are defined by Jesus in us—always full of His grace and power—there are times where all of us seem to have a lot of trouble accessing it. This can go on for years.

Sometimes after I speak, there are those who will scold me, "John, how dare you say such a thing? You're a child of the king. Royalty. You are not a ragamuffin, nor any other lesser distinction." I hear that. I know that I am His, with Christ fully in me, and that I'm not defined by any lesser title. But being a child of the King doesn't automatically make me mature. Even with Jesus Christ's very person living in me, I still carry strangeness from choices I made early on, and even some that others made before me. But if I'm only allowed to declare that I'm a prince or a princess of the King, triumphant over all sin and such, I just get forced into more skillful hiding. I believe it might be better to give answers to God's children—His princes and princesses—who find they're still capable of lies, deception, jealousy, depression, vanity, hiding, hypocrisy, and all manner of sin. These are the specific children of God that I find myself writing to now. Hopefully, my thoughts express to you what our Father would want you to know.

You are as precious to Me at this very moment, as any human who has ever walked the earth.

For Me to fix everything would not be to care for you. To give you what you envy of others would not be to love you well, but instead, to leave you unhealthy. To heal every infirmity would never allow you to learn dependence upon Me, or enter into compassion for others. It would never satisfy your heart, or allow My glory to be revealed in you.

The best and greatest life is not the pristine life, the fully satiated life, the fixed life, or the neatly ordered life. The best life is the real one, where I receive glory as you trust Me, enjoy Me, and enjoy others, amidst the beauty and the rubble.

I refashion all the evil on this planet, which hits every one of you, and actually employ it to move you to maturity, and give you an even better life than if it had never happened.

Which is a better life? To falsely appear good, but be hidden and not really trusted or known? Or instead, to be authentic, trusted, loved, and known, though you fail? Your spouse and friends are praying you will choose the latter, even with all the failure and revealing it carries with it. If you don't, they will never have the opportunity to know and trust you entirely.

Loss of a present sense of My love is not the same as the loss of My love itself.

The goal of the Christian life is not in what you can produce for Me, but rather by learning to depend upon Me in what you cannot produce.

A relationship of love is formed most deeply, not when you are on your game, but when you can't seem to make sense of almost anything.

You are already as righteous as you will ever be. Nothing in you will ever heal because you attempt to become more holy or righteous.

When you can't feel My affection, it is never because I am angry or disappointed with you.

Whatever condition it is in yourself that you hate, I have known of it from before the world began. My love is not dependent on your improvement. It is the real you I love, not the you that you think you should be.

The love of My Son Jesus is never being withheld from you. He is loving you with all He is, every moment of every day. He went to the cross so He could be endlessly close to you—even if that thing you hate in yourself never improves.

I wanted, and still want, an exact you, for this exact time in human history, for those I've prepared for you. I love you exactly who I made you to be. I love the one I created—exactly as you were created. Yes, your response to the Fall has created patterns, and all manner of confusion, but it cannot change the definition of the person I delighted in creating. Nothing about you was a mistake. And those things you dislike about your physical imperfections, even those, I will use wonderfully.

2017

HOW DO I describe playful, God-centered freedom? I can't. I only know I stumbled into it. And that it is the reason I will make it through the storms I am faced with.

For a while, I was the most sold-out, diligent, religious guy you'd ever meet. But I was miserable. Few are more miserable than a religiously miserable person. These days, I may become sad, confused, or bewildered—but I've never been that miserable guy from my past again. There is something about knowing for certain, that God is absolutely delighted with your very being, that changes everything.

You can't speed up the process of believing your complete acceptance. You can't speed up the process of believing you're adored. You can't speed up the process of believing you are righteous—that He lives in you—that you don't need to become someone you think you're supposed to be. You can't speed up the process of believing you're not behind. You can't speed up the process of believing you're enough and right on time. You can't speed up the process of believing you don't have to add a thing. You can't speed up the process of letting go of trying to maintain your good Christian testimony. You can't speed up the process of not listening to internal, or external, shame-filled voices that prod you into something short of obedience. You can't speed up the process of believing that you actually get to relax, enjoy, and love whatever God puts in front of you.

But as you journey through these processes and begin to form this new way of believing, an entire way of seeing God's very nature is uniquely time-released throughout your whole being. Everything begins to be viewed differently. Pain is still pain, glare is still glare, loss is still gut-wrenching. But you are free. So you play differently. You dream differently. You love differently. You relax differently. You affirm differently. You bless differently. You receive differently. You love unbelievers instead of pitying them—or envying them. You begin to believe that the world will change, not by desperately trying to fix it, but by loving it, by enjoying it, and by being exactly who He made you to be in it.

This means my sometimes random, non-sequitur, free association is not random to God. My laughter and unhurried enjoyment is sacred. Giving dignity to my past is sacred. This means a horribly devastated world need not always devastate me. This means I don't always have to feel like I have to do more. It means drawing closer to those who fail. It means allowing others to draw close to me when I fail. It is finding others and entering in with them, having no fear of the consequences if the relationship doesn't last. It means appealing to Christ-in-me to grow healthier, instead of vigilantly trying to fix myself. It means risking love and being willing to be naively fooled. It means giving up an agenda for others' lives. It means convincing those I influence that there is no other shoe about to drop. It means believing I have a new heart and giving myself the benefit of the doubt when it comes to my motives. It means living as one who needs to impress no one, and yet finds great joy in pleasing everyone. It means allowing Jesus to correct me and direct me, without hearing a voice of displeasure. It means daring to take a risk on something and trusting that God will come through. It means dreaming big and knowing He won't try to teach me a lesson if I fall short.

June, 2017

APPARENTLY, NOT EVERYONE likes me. I discovered this in 2017 when I became aware that there were those around me who resented me, disdained me, and were actually working against me. One particular June day, someone chose to vomit judgments all over me, in a verbally-violent, belittling, humiliating tirade. I have no memory of how I got home that day, and little memory of the days following. I've since learned that while we each face trauma in different ways, there are some inviolable consistencies. Apparently, if we get hit with a flood of unexpected stimuli, too fast and too intense, our central decision-making system makes the call that we've hit emotional and cognitive overload. Our mind makes an instant decision to switch over to a back-up operating system. Almost involuntarily, we are kindly rushed from the reasonable, deft, and nuanced thinking part of our brain, to a region more blunt, rigid, and unreasoning. Thoughts now come in short, staccato bursts. Memory is put in selective and protective lock-down. Reason shuts down as you enter survival mode. And survival mode only gives you three ways to move forward: flight, fight, or freeze. I froze. And it would take the rest of that year, and most of the next, for me to begin to thaw out.

At my best, I am innocently playful, absurd, and lead with

self-deprecating humor. If someone is not endeared to me, I give a lot of ammo for them to attack me. But I never thought anyone hated me. How could they? I'm, well, I'm me! I don't wish anything bad for anyone—except maybe for arrogant abusers and those who brag like they've earned the fortune they inherited.

I've typically seen myself as beloved, enjoyed, and needed. It has carried me through pain, loss, rejection, and the insecurity my family line has passed down. But on that June day in 2017, my very person was attacked. The way I lived, the way I spoke, the way I carried myself, the way I communicated, my integrity, and the motives for everything I did. I was attacked, demeaned, and mocked. It suddenly challenged everything I had built my playful innocence upon. Evil had done its homework. All I could do in those moments was attempt to survive the onslaught. All I could think was, *How do I get this to stop?* My attempts weren't working. The man I was speaking with continued to spit out words, "Don't give me that look, you phony! See, you're making that little smirk you do. It makes me sick to my stomach. No! Don't try to talk. Just shut up and hear the real truth about yourself. Now, you're doing that thing with your eyes. Shut up and take this, you fake!"

I don't know if there was anything I could have done in those moments that would have been seen as normal to him. If I screwed up and made the wrong expression, I thought he might physically attack me. Only later, when my normal operating system was rebooting, did I feel the real damage of his attack. The feeling of being the phony he has accused me of being. All my insecurities broke through the door of faith and flooded over the definition I had of myself. It was astonishing how quickly my perception of myself had become so perilously vulnerable.

Am I completely deceived about who I am? Am I incapable of thinking clearly and objectionably about myself? Why has no one else ever told me these things before? Is he saying what others have always wanted to say? Am I someone so sick and weak, that friends have had to artificially build me up and never speak negatively into my life issues? Have I been annoying or even angering to others when I thought I was such a damned gift? (Faithlessness apparently swears.) Deep sigh.

I realize as I write this I'm probably describing more than just me. Most of us have experienced something similar. But some have gone through it alone, and are still trudging on, trying to make sense of life in their new normal. A new normal with a limp.

Maybe this chapter is a re-awakening of your own version of trauma. Perhaps formed by verbal abuse, sexual abuse, shocking violence, watching harm inflicted onto those you love, sudden loss, failure, hateful ridicule, etc. Evil comes in so many forms. In my case, evil studied my life, found the exact set of words that would cause the most damage to my soul, and spewed doubt all over the John Lynch I thought I knew. Maybe I wasn't Christ in me after all. Maybe I wasn't really changed after all. Maybe those were just hyperbolic sentiments. Maybe I was only a saved, disappointing sinner. I felt so naked, exposed, betrayed, and full of incriminating self-doubt. I wish I could give you the comfort that my life eventually went back to normal. But I'd be lying to you. There was no going back to what once was.

I still may not be fully healed from what happened that day but I truly think I'm healthier, stronger, more honest, more compassionate, and far more trusting of God to reflect His view of me and how I'm affecting others. I discovered that I needed a much stronger conviction of who I was; built on more than presumptions, half-truths, adulation, or an idealized sense of self. The journey to uncover this led me to incredible, real hope. Hope that I now get to impart to you.

The Awakening I'm about to share with you has been the prologue on my journey to that new home. I hope some of you will put them on your refrigerator, or bedroom mirror, for the times when lies creep in under the wire causing you to doubt yourself and question if you were ever truly made new.

. . . Awakening . . .

No human, good or bad in their intent, gets to define me. I am no longer my perceived shame, but instead, a new creature—Jesus in me—holy, righteous, clean, beloved, and intentionally planned for. Not only judicially, forensically, or theologically, but actually. For real, in this very moment.

This irreducibly constant identity has been objectively, uniquely, and unbreakably formed—not by my successes or effort, but on my behalf, by the very God of the universe! He made me perfectly, the way He wanted me. I have a chosen personality and how I influence the world delights Him daily; even on the days when I can do no more than hide in bed. I have not been revealed as a phony, nor am I insufficient, no matter what has been said about me, and no matter by how many. I am enough. Surpassingly enough. He has endued me with distinctively needed goodness, perspective, and a way of expressing life for the benefit of others. That I have yet to tap into all of this completely is irrelevant. There is wonder He will release through me in coming chapters of my life that will leave me breathless and full of praise. Believing this is ultimately the way home from distortion, humiliation, and a shattered heart.

July 21, 2017

I WOKE UP in the middle of it. The first thing I remembered was asking Stacey to tell me that she loved me. It seemed to me a very important request. I wonder if, in those moments, I sensed I might be dying.

Stacey looked over at me and asked, more as a joke, "What's with the mumbling and slurring? Are you having a stroke?" Turns out I was.

The next thing I remember I was sitting in our sunroom. I attempted to set my coffee mug back onto the table and missed... badly. It landed with a hard thud, spilling coffee in every direction. Stacey asked me to read a section from The Message. She's a speech therapist and wanted to hear my speech. I got frustrated and walked to the bedroom to change from pajamas into my shorts. My plan was to take a walk. Stacey had seen, and heard, enough. She quickly pulled up Google and typed "What to do if someone is having a stroke."

Meanwhile, it was taking me several dozen tries to get my right foot into my shorts. For some reason, this didn't alarm me. I vaguely remember emerging from the bedroom to hear Stacey ask, "Is that how you want to look going to the hospital? Because we're going *right* now." That was the last thing I remembered for a while.

We arrived at the hospital. There was no one in the emergency room that Monday morning. They took me in immediately, like I was the Duke of Monrovia. Soon a team of six or seven people were working on me. The trauma team at St. Joseph's was exceptional. In such settings, I have an almost involuntary need to be chatty and funny. I guess I wanted everyone to know I was ok. But no one was responding to a thing I was saying. And I was tossing out what were, in my opinion, some very funny lines.

Soon, I was wheeled to the MRI room. The technician was having none of my cleverness. Before I could get my first punch line out, she interrupted, "That's nice, honey. Let's try to be a bit less talkative so I can explain what we're about to do." Talk about a tough crowd.

Back in my room, I realized I was starving. Thankfully, Kali and Caleb called to ask what they could bring for me before coming to the hospital. I requested two Taco Bell burritos and one crunchy taco. They were spectacular. Minutes later, a nurse kindly instructed me to be sure I didn't eat any food until I was given the swallowing test I needed, later in the day. "Yes, of course, no food..." I responded while hoping there was no cheese in my beard. Kali, meanwhile, quietly placed the remnants of my Taco Bell indulgence behind her. Turned out, I'd dodged a bullet.

Later, a doctor entered my room. He told us that my stroke was at the tip of the highest sapling, at the very apex of the tree. It had hit grey matter. Following the doctor's report, I made the mistake of commenting, "So, basically, you're saying I'm pretty much like everyone else?"

"Oh no, Mr. Lynch. Not at all," he deadpanned. "From here on out, you're a person who creates strokes. Period. Have a good day, sir." Nothing like a doctor with a gentle bedside manner.

You never truly realize how much you are loved by your friends until you scare them. You can't use it often, but in moderation it really is incredible. I would gradually forget most of the promises I made about changing the tension of my lifestyle, but I would not forget the love and care that was shown by friends around me, my virtual friends, and even friends I had lost touch with for years.

I was released on Thursday. On Friday, I sat with our senior pastor and Caleb, attempting to convince them that I had recovered sufficiently enough to preach that coming Sunday. We were at the end of Ecclesiastes chapter two. Getting to preach that passage was the reason I had picked the book so many months before; I couldn't miss my chance. It's odd to watch others study you as you try to appear normal enough to be allowed to do what you long to do. Whatever I did worked. I preached, and the world continued to spin.

People often ask me what I think I've lost due to the stroke. It usually feels like a trick question. Like they're thinking, "I can see two dozen things he's lost. I just want to see if he's self-aware, or if he's lost that too?"

One of my best friends, Steve Larson, is a speech pathologist who works with people who've had a stroke. He and his wife, Grace, came to our home during that first week to encourage us and ensure our hearts that I would, in fact, be okay. He said he couldn't see any damage at all. I believe I've lost some capacity. It takes me nearly twice as long to accomplish half as much. And I'm aware that I'm often forced to use a handful of ten-dollar words because I'm no longer able to come up with fifty-dollar ones. Stacey believes what I've lost most is my confidence. She's usually right about such things.

The truth is, I don't feel as sharp on stage as I once did. Two cruises back, with MercyMe, I was giving the "Two Roads" talk during the evening session. Giving this talk is like ordering a piece of pie—I've done it at least five hundred times before. But that time I got lost. I walked out a door I should have gone into, and suddenly I didn't know how to move forward. I was absolutely lost. Inside, I was yelling in panic, *God, what just happened? Where am I? Help! I have to keep speaking, but I have no idea where I am in the talk. I'm scared.*

I sensed Him saying,

Well, this is an unusual turn of events. Ok. First, calm down, John. Take a deep breath—you're great at this. I think you may have inverted a section so, let's get out of this part and move to the crossroads. If you appear confident, some in the audience might wonder if they missed something, and instead, they'll blame themselves for not paying better attention.

Stacey told me later that as she listened to me from her seat in the middle of the audience, she was panicking, thinking, *Oh shoot. This is bad. Really bad. This is going to be our last cruise!* She's a bit pragmatic.

Back in our room, Stacey said all the right things. But I started to cry. "Stacey, I feel like an old prizefighter. I used to be sharp and could handle any setting. My words and memory could punch myself out of any situation. But now I'm taking hits. Straight on. I'm afraid of getting embarrassed, of embarrassing you. I'm afraid of God kindly needing to remove me from the stage." These moments are where Stacey is at her best with me. She does not sugar-coat anything but she believes in me so much. She believes I am, at 68 percent, better than most communicators at 100 percent.

So, I have kept moving forward, trying to distinguish between the limitation of old age and the damage incurred that morning of July 21st, 2017. One thing I know for certain is that since that day, I have not been able to say "Disneyland" without bumbling it. Even now, I still struggle saying it. But I can live with that. Heck, we can always go to Knott's Berry Farm instead.

On My Worst Day

February
2018

IT HAD BEEN eight months… Eight months since I froze.

My birthday was approaching. February 16th. My 65th. For the first time, I really didn't want it celebrated. I'd had many incredibly memorable birthday celebrations. But at this time, I was still shattered; unable, or perhaps unwilling, to crawl out of the hole someone else had dug for me. The last thing I wanted was for my friends and family to mail this one in—planning a party for me out of some kindness or obligation. I had no interest in celebrating the shell of my former self I had become.

I was in a lot of pain from my neuropathy. My feet, often uncontrollably, felt as though they were on fire. I'd purchased a medical marijuana card but was too afraid to use it. The level of THC it would take for the pain I was experiencing to recede would make me stoned like a chihuahua on peyote berries. I was already taking eight potent drugs to keep myself moderately in the game. I didn't need gummy-bear weed to space me out and cause me to stare into my refrigerator all day.

On this particular birthday, I wanted to be given the permission to drive, all by myself, to San Diego, so I could sit on a hotel balcony with a blanket over my knees, and look out over the Crystal Pier cottages, Mission Beach, and Pacific Ocean. But, honestly, even that sounded like a lot of work.

I was exceedingly *not* alright. I'd lost my confidence, my humor, my message, my place in space. And I'm not even certain I knew what "my place in space" meant, I just knew I wasn't certain of where, or if, I fit anymore.

Then it happened. A series of events, with an outcome that, in the condition I was in, I would never have believed was possible.

It all started one day in late January, with me simply noticing a nice, new wicker basket sitting outside our front door. Stacey observed me noticing our new home decor and said, "You're not going to believe what your daughter, Amy, has done. That's all I'm going to say." And when Stacey tells you "that's all" she's going to say, there is no need to bother continuing the conversation—she's not going to tell you!

On February 1st, Stacey mentioned that there was something in the basket out on our porch and that I should go out to get it. It was a gift and note from Amy and her husband, Cody. Few love, care for, and advocate for those around them like our Amy. People are changed through the gift of her in their lives. I am one of those people. Her note read, "Dad, you are the most beloved human I know. No one loves you more than me. I know you are hurting. I want you to see that you have an army of friends surrounding you. They have your back. Each day, for the rest of this month, there will be a gift in this basket for you along with a letter from some of your best friends in this world. Forgive me for those I've missed. You have friends everywhere that I've yet to meet. I can't wait for you to read the letters about what your friendship has meant to the people in your life and the impact you've had on them. I've gotten to read them all. You will be a wreck by the 6th! I love you so much. Your first letter is from me, Cody, Ridge, and Navy. I'm so grateful my kids get to have you as their grandfather."

She went on to speak about our relationship in a way that made me feel like the most important person on the planet. I was devastated, in the best possible way. I began to cry like someone who's watched a batch of old home movies.

And just as Amy said, each day, without fail, I woke up to find a gift and a letter in the basket. Each one crushed me with goodness. Many of the best friends I have on the planet, told me how my life had changed theirs. They shared stories and anecdotes, and each expressed a love that caused me to shake my head back and forth in stunned gratitude, limply dangling the letter at my side as I stared out into space.

They kept coming. One day, one note, one gift spilling into the next, forming the unique tapestry of the life God had given me. And through each, God Himself poured out the delight He has for me.

I once attended the memorial service of a woman in her nineties. She was an incredible human. But all her friends had long since passed. Those at the service were her family, and the children and grandchildren of her lifelong friends. It got me thinking; there is definitely an optimal time to leave this earth. What if we could pick the terms and timing of another's blessing into our lives? What if, instead of waiting until we had left this earth, we had the opportunity to hear the impact our lives had on others while there was still time for it to change us?

I love the tender Irish comedy, *Waking Ned Devine*. In it, two lifelong friends, O'Shea and O'Sullivan, discover their friend Ned Devine has died of a heart attack upon hearing he won the national lottery. Since Devine is the only one who can claim the prize, the townspeople try to trick the claim inspector into believing that O'Sullivan is Devine. They put on a wake for O'Sullivan. It unknowingly gives the townsfolk the opportunity to bless his life while O'Sullivan hides from the claim inspector behind a curtain. Most of us might secretly wish we could stand behind a curtain to hear our best friends give our eulogy while we're still in the middle of our journeys—to get to hear our best friends tell the best about us before we're gone. That February, I got to experience my eulogy. We can do similar versions of this for our friends and family, from God, at any time.

At some point, later in that month, I was finally convinced of this one singular thought from God:

John, you can no longer hold onto the lie that you are not loved, known, or important. You've seen too much now. Your friends are not making this stuff up. They are intentionally and vulnerably pouring out their hearts to you—for you—and it will change you. Yes, you will still get afraid sometimes. You will still question if you have the message a particular group needs. The doubts may still come to you in different forms, but you'll be able to lean into what you've heard from Me this month. I have made an indelible mark on this planet with you, My child. You may no longer spin the story any other way. It will no longer work for you, even on your worst day.

It would be, and continues to be, all borrowed time from here on out. Nothing could be able to top that revelation from God to me. As the last day of the month approached, I asked if I could continue receiving letters for the rest of the year. Even if we had to rent people! I didn't need any more gifts, I just wanted those notes.

My grandchildren saw me open many of those gifts and watched tears run down my cheeks as I read the notes that came with each.

They cherished what they observed taking place in me—for me, their grandfather. What they saw impacted them. Soon they began wrapping gifts, things from around our home, and placing them into the wicker basket. Along with each gift was a note. Oh, how love changes those it impacts.

February 28th, late in the evening, I had this thought: *Hmm... Well, dang. Would you look at that... I'm no longer shattered. That season of self-pity, self-doubt, and self-protection seems to now be over. Believed affirmation really does what I've been promising it does.*

As I was taught by my friend and hero, Bill Thrall, "Affirmation never puffs up the believer. Instead, it humbles, and causes them to want to do more of what they've been affirmed for, in the setting that did the affirming." When March 1st came, I humbly set off to bless all those who had affirmed me—those who kindly and lovingly reminded me of who I had forgotten I was. Since that time, I have never stopped seeking out those who desperately need this truth too.

2018

HENRI NOUWEN WRITES these profound words in *Letters to Marc About Jesus*. "A lot of people have to expend so much energy on overcoming their low opinion of themselves that they seldom get round to asking about the purpose of their existence. And if they do, it is often out of fear."[3]

He is, of course, correct. Learning who we are in Christ serves more than to free us from shame. It is, of course, that—beautifully that—but the end game of apprehending grace and identity is for the privilege of entering into what we were put on earth to live out. We may call it destiny or simply living well, but ultimately, our pleasure, joy, and delight cannot come through seeking after them. Rather, they are a by-product of allowing this beautiful expression of Christ in us to be played out. This quote has helped me realize anew why I am so compelled to promote these truths of our identity in Christ. Our vision must be to help others discover, not just what they were freed from, but the wonder they've been freed into!

This revelation has created within me even more urgency to live out of my identity in Christ. It gives me courage to ask the life-giving questions which can only be asked when I am no longer fighting to prove I am enough, or hiding the behaviors I fear will confirm I am not enough. It is when we end that fool's game, that beautiful questions can emerge.

God, who do I get to express Your love to today?

God, who has been waiting for me to love them well? God, how can I receive Your love, wildly and endlessly?

God, how do I best love those who don't know You?

God, what destiny and dreams are You forming in my heart?

God, who needs me to stand with them in a vision You have given them?

God, who can help me to mature into my destiny?

God, who can I help to mature into their destiny?

God, what brings my heart great joy?

God, what do we do best together?

I don't want to miss the beauty of what He has for me to live out. I missed the pleasure of that for far too long.

2018

OUR AUDITORIUM WAS packed and electric that Sunday morning of 2018. The elders were going to announce Open Door Fellowship's new lead pastor. We'd been searching for so long. Finally, with friends and family all bunched together, the elders announced that Caleb Lynch would be our new lead pastor! The place exploded in wild approval. I hadn't seen such celebration in that community for a long, long time.

I don't want to harm this beautiful narrative by giving the painful backstory. It's one that I don't even have the ability to explain. I tried to write that story for you. I couldn't do it. I'm not sure I even understand most of what happened in that season. I do know that it was dark. Open Door went through our toughest and saddest season from 2016-2018. Caleb offered himself at the very start of that ugly time. Two years later, in 2018, we all knew that God had him waiting for us all along. We were still fragile from those two years, but we were now finding each other again and remembering why we made our way into this community in the first place.

Caleb is not only my son, he is one of my very best friends. I know him exceedingly well. But this wise and capacious man I was now watching lead Open Door—this man who was loving the staff so beautifully, who was giving vision to our community, who was preaching so far over his head... That man, I was not nearly as familiar with him. I'm almost certain he grew up in our home. But, God's hand was, and continues to be, fully and supernaturally upon *this* man, at *this* certain time, for *this* particular group of people.

Caleb became an exceptionally trusted, compassionate, uber-competent, Christ-centered leader. A man who has loved this community with all his heart, his entire life. His humility and stable, God-trusting passion has brought him to this moment in our history.

Bill Thrall invested so much in me so that one day I would help lead this community. As wise as he is, even Bill couldn't have known. It was my son that Open Door was truly waiting for. It was my son who would help to rebuild this community and to free us into a new iteration of this life in grace. I once asked him, during a particularly hard time back in 2016, "Caleb, you've seen us at our worst. Why would you want to become a leader at Open Door?" He answered, "Dad, I've seen too much to go back to anything else. I can take the downside because I've witnessed the upside. I grew up in an environment of health and life, in our family and in this community. This is the one place I have to protect."

Nothing makes me happier than hearing someone say, "Hey, you're Caleb Lynch's dad, aren't you? Your voice sounds like his. You're his dad, right?" I smile and nod my head, "Why, yes. Yes, I am."

2019

I HAVE HEARD people say, usually indirectly, "If he's able to write and speak so confidently about identity in Christ, how can he describe himself as being so insecure?" Fair question. Truly, more than fair. I think my answer these days would be: Maybe I don't understand what the heck I'm talking about. Or maybe I'm a fake. Or maybe what I'm talking and writing about doesn't really work, after all. Or maybe, just maybe, I have been placed perfectly, exactly where I am on this journey, by a sovereign God, who knows my particular starting points, my generational lineage, my woundings, the things done to me, the things I've done to others, and the crippling moments of horror that perhaps the critics have not seen. Whatever the case, though, God is addressing my immaturity in His perfect and satisfying order. I am, after all, by definition of my God's control, right on time. I am perfectly maturing as I carry at once both His actual righteousness and His very being dwelling in me.

With all of that said, I'm able to trust my motives only about 57 percent of the time. (Note that this is up from 32 percent, which is where it was two years into my ride with Jesus. I have the stats if you'd like to see them.) Look, I can't judge anyone, let alone myself. I don't have the chops. But I know that He wildly wanted a "me" on this planet, at this time, even with all these, as yet, unresolved and perceived failings.

If we turn grace into a formula with a timetable and a picture of what we're supposed to look like after a certain time, then we are not that different from those with the moralistic belief that our worth and value are determined by how much fruit we've produced. And that just leads to focusing on which fruit and how much fruit and how quickly we can produce it. I'll be absolutely ruined if I revert to that system. Jesus is truly all I have anymore. I have no other source of goodness to grow any faster into who I would like to be. So, I would imagine you would have to take up your concerns about me with Him. Because I can't figure me out either. Here's my guess: there are aspects of the fruit of the Spirit of God that He has disproportionately developed in me. And they are a gift to many. It makes me shake my head and smile with joyous gratefulness. But I wonder if there are places of blinding, and blinded, failure in me that I will carry to the grave. I never want to use this as an excuse, a self-entitlement, or a pass for any wrong in me. I hate that these things rob me of permission into more people's lives. But I do know this: I am fused perfectly with Christ. He adores me and even on my worst day, I have only His redeeming and sanctifying love to count on. This is the power of the cross and resurrection.

Oh, and He knows where to find me. He's right here within me, as close as my next breath. I am coming to be vitally good with this. My immaturity is flamboyant, I'll give you that. Another's immaturity might not be. But everyone carries their own measure of immaturity. If you think you have developed a formula to grow up faster than "trusting God with me and others", knock yourself out. There are no "together" people. Just those wonderfully carrying the person of Jesus in their being; gradually and sweetly maturing into who we actually already are. I'll ride that train all night long and into the morning until the steward kindly gives me a warm towel, juice, and a croissant.

2019

THE VOICE CAN be so brilliantly and logically crafted that we can presume everything it tells us is coming from God. The negative messages it whispers all play into the haunting shame that wove its way into our being before we became new. Will the way we've chosen to see God really hold up? Will trusting our identity in Christ alone really be enough? The thought of returning to pretending we are enough can scare us. We forget that we already are enough.

That voice mocks us: *Well, here you are. You trusted that your new heart would be drawn to God and that it would be enough. But look at you now... You feel distant and you're not on fire for God. Admit it. The good news is, it's not too late. You can build systems back up, follow technique, and garner self-effort to care enough. You know He's disappointed with where you are now. Just admit that the whole grace thing doesn't work. Then come back to the accurate mistrust of yourself and get back on track. Left to yourself you won't care enough about God. You know that, right? You wanted to play hooky and now look where it's gotten you. You got your hand caught in the cookie jar. You've had your fun.*

So, here's the game plan. You need a season of really working at it;

a season of striving and convincing Him that you care enough. That's what He wants. Besides, if this is the best of the Christian life, well then, how do you explain the dryness? You know you feel closest to Him when you're proving to Him that you want Him enough, right? Let go of that crazy talk that it's more important to let Him love you than you loving Him enough. You know what will bring things back in line; a little self-disgust and a little begging to feel something more. You see them, those sold-out ones, right? It's a lot of work and self-effort, but that feeling of almost getting there is worth it.

Stop. Enough! That ship has sailed—but not before it almost killed us. Many of us already found ourselves washed up on the shore of cynical, jaded disillusionment.

God is not afraid to risk the consequences of what we do with His grace. Many fear that if grace is preached we will take advantage of it and head straight to the dog track with an armload of Johnny Walker and cartons of off-brand cigarettes. They may be forgetting that we have a new nature—Jesus in us. The most real us does not want to get away with anything. God will take His chances with the power of grace to heal us, free us, and defeat the issues of sin because He knows the alternative does only the opposite.

What if we believed that we were fused together with God—that we were inseparable? What if He was in charge of the timing of our maturity, our intimacy, and our playful delight in each other? What if we could lean on that?

What if we gave ourselves permission to be thirsty, and then allowed Him to slake that thirst, instead of working so hard to avoid thirst? After all, when we're not thirsty, all liquid is tolerable if doctored up enough. But a cold drink of water when you're thirsty?... That might be one of the top experiences you get on this planet.

What if we could rest in the reality that He has not gone anywhere and that He has wired us to want Him, and to be wanted by Him? "I have been crucified with Christ; and it is no longer I who live, but Christ lives in me; and the *life* which I now live in the flesh I live by faith in the Son of God, who loved me and gave Himself up for me" Galatians 2:20 (NASB). If this verse is true, then that ridiculous religious game of getting fired up enough to care is over. If you are willing to take the gamble that the absolute desire and longing to love, and be loved by Him in infinite measure, is within you, well then, you will begin to enjoy an incredible experience.

Don't be freaked out by less than ecstatic seasons of life. Just like any relationship, your relationship with Him is taking its perfect course. So, relax, rest, stay, enjoy, trust, and enter in deeply with Him, simply because you want to. Soon, you'll find yourself living this way easily because... well, because you won't want to not live this way. You will know and believe the truth that there is no life in these disciplines, but rather, the disciplines were graciously given by God as the vehicle for you to go play with the one you are wired to want. You get to stop beating yourself up. You have that right as a child of God's. Go, trust your new heart. Have a ball! This is a small glimpse of what it means to have Christ in you.

2019

WHEN SHE WAS young, my daughter Carly and I would find any excuse to go on drives together to make up wonderful, little, non-sequitur rhyming songs. We made ourselves laugh so hard. In this very book, there's a chapter from 2001 that contains a few of our greatest hits.

In her teens, Carly became our family theologian. She loved to study critical commentaries and parse original languages. Next, she became our social activist and progressive defender of those without a voice. She did her post-degree studies in theological faith responses to trauma at Boston University. She is currently the diversity campus pastor at Santa Clara University and leads vigils for communities of Jews, Muslims, and Christians. She never loses her kindness and always offers respectful love to all who cross her path.

Mostly joking, I often say that of all three of my children I am only certain that I am Carly's father. My DNA in her is so obvious—in all the best and hardest ways. Regardless, she has surpassed me in all the best ways. If I am a gifted communicator—she is more gifted. If I am funny—she is funnier. If I am intelligent—she is more intelligent. If I understand kindness and the issues of the heart—Carly lives them out in more maturity than me. If I can articulate political positions— she does it more cogently than me. If I know how to care for the wounded or suffering—she does it with more care than me. That may all sound unnecessarily self-deprecating unless you're fortunate to spend an evening with her. Then, you just might add several more items to this list.

During the weeks before and after Carly left for Azusa Pacific University, I remember playing a particular song over and over. Maybe it was because she was our last one to leave home, or maybe it was because she and I were connected so deeply by the way we both saw life. Maybe it was because I knew she was not an extrovert and wondered if she might struggle in those first few months when extro- verts rule the scene. Whatever the reason, the song was on repeat.

For me, the chorus was saying that wherever Carly found herself, if she needed me, I'd walk anywhere to get to her.

And then, she was gone.

Somewhere in her time studying theology and social justice she began to see things differently than me. For most of our lives together we'd always talked through our similar understandings. Almost every night I was home during her childhood, I would lay next to her before bed and think through everything, both the important or the nearly nonsensical. Now suddenly, she had a community and professors whose voices were becoming louder than mine. I suppose you somehow hope that your children will independently form their own way of seeing and articulating their own convictions that are built on the shoulders of what you taught and the values you modeled for them. The hardest part for me was that I was experiencing her autonomy not only as a father but as her pastor. In the course of a year Carly was coming home with less confidence in some of the truths I'd raised her in, and more confidence in truths I either did not yet understand or did not espouse.

I can remember exactly where I was sitting the afternoon we got into it. She was home on break. She didn't know how to express what she was learning without hurting me. I didn't know how to respond to what she was learning without hurting her. Both happened. Looking back, it was my own insecurity and fear that caused me to say things that have taken a long time for her to contextualize and release me from. It started out innocuously. Carly was explaining a type of worship service on campus that she had come to appreciate. Instead of listening, asking, and reasoning, in essence, I demanded a loyalty check from her. *How could she not agree with me? I'm her dad! I've written books, I've given talks; I've been in a movie for crying out loud! Who are these teachers filling her head with new ways of seeing*

Scripture?

It took me several years to realize that I had been childish. But I had lost my daughter's trust and vulnerability for longer than that. The last several years I had to learn how to earn back trust I violated with someone so sacredly dear to me. At some point I had to ask myself, *Is it more important that I get to enjoy, and be enjoyed, by my daughter regardless of what she believes, or for me to be proven right and lose her heart?*

We were never anything like estranged. She always knew my love, and I knew hers. But Carly waited for her dad to grow up. And I had to wait for her to see that I was growing up.

Then one day, there was a voice message from her. It was so tender and humble—owning her part and expressing how much she desired me to be close to her in her life. Not too long afterward, we got to talk on the phone for a long, unhurried, playful time. That time was filled with remembered delight, safety, and open hands. We both were fully melted.

Carly and I both will likely always carry theological, cultural, and social convictions the other does not. Some might tell me that I should keep aggressively forcing the argument until she agrees with me. But that ship has sailed. She is not in a "phase." She is not going to agree with me the more she grows up. She is grown up. She carries so many beautiful convictions and she gives me permission to carry convictions differing from hers, without it interfering with our love for each other. And I'm still growing. When it comes to faith and political and cultural issues, my views and practices are transforming in ways I would not have considered twenty years ago.

If I am going to have any significant influence in Carly's life, it will be as a curious learner. She already knows what I believe. She grew up in it. But she wants to know that I want to know what she believes.

And because it is my Carly who holds these positions, I care deeply about learning her motivations, convictions, and values.

It is tough to learn to love our children well during all seasons and to allow them to love us well in return. We can fear that if we admit wrong, or are found in error, that we'll lose their respect. But in truth, I'm learning there is no amount of admitting wrong that will take their respect away. We only lose their respect when we are too proud, or too afraid, to admit our own failures, weaknesses, or inadequacies.

I love, enjoy, and respect Carly so much. And while I am her dad, we are now two adults. In so many ways she has become my peer. I am being let back in—and I won't go out there again.

On my last birthday, a post showed up on Facebook from Carly. It included a photo that Carly had taken of me out on our patio—a place where we have sat by the fireplace with glasses of wine in hand talking about politics, theology, music, comedians, and places we have visited, more times than I can count.

And then she wrote these words above that photo: "Apart from Stacey Lynch, there is no one who has gotten to stand and stare at this view as many times as I have. And it's all because of that sweet man there on the left. He has an inability to keep good wine to himself. He also lacks the capacity to ignore the pain in others. He is the kindest man, with the most love for a golden retriever that I have ever known. Every year that I discover a new thing about myself that is undeniably his genes (even the fragile, insecure, spiraling tornado of doubt parts), I can't help but be endlessly thankful that I am his daughter. John Lynch, thank you for your loving words and the salve they place on my hurting heart on the hardest of days. Thank you for your unmatchable humor that is only ever used for good. Thank you for loving me fiercely, even in the seasons I have been distant. I love you. I love you. I love you. And I miss you more than I knew I could. Happy birthday, sweetest Daddo!"

August 20th, 2019

BALI PASSED AWAY on August 20th, 2019. Our incredible golden retriever gave us sixteen years. I know that most dog owners think that theirs is incredible—but Bali truly, almost never, did anything wrong. If she did, she wore it like a faithful penitent at the height of Lent.

I sincerely believe that the reason she lived far past her time was to protect me. When I was diagnosed with neuropathy, she would no longer allow me to climb ladders. She had no issues with ladders before. What dog does that? And while ladders were suddenly off-limits to me, she would still let me work with power tools without so much as a yelp. I think she was trying to say, "Master, look, I think we've established your feet don't work and yet, you want to climb a ladder to wrap a strand of lights around a pole standing high on our roof? No, see, that's not going to happen. Not on my watch. Now, get down or I'll keep barking. You can take me inside, but you will still hear me bark and we both know, it'll break your heart. So, it's your call. We can either fold that ladder back up, or your favorite dog is about to lose her voice."

I'm grateful God took her home when He did. She was almost

unable to stand for several weeks leading up to that August day. On the day of her heart attack, she stumbled into my office to find me right before it happened. As we waited for the vet to show up, I gave her whipped cream from my hand and stroked her fur as I reminded her of all we'd shared together. I put the phone to her ear to let her hear Carly's voice all the way in California. And then, with the doctor's second injection, my hero went to sleep; home with her Creator.

In some ways, I think loving a dog well is more necessary than loving a human well. Hear me out...

If I pass away, Stacey will grieve—she really likes me. But she'll get along just fine. She's pretty self-sufficient and competent. She'll probably get remarried within a couple of months to a guy with a pencil-thin moustache. A guy who will likely spend my retirement on a vintage accordion and cases of thin, reedy Pinot Noir.

But if it were just Bali and I left together and I checked out, Bali would be helpless. She cannot make her way in the world. She was totally dependent upon me being a good and caring man. That's why the love from a dog is so heart-wrenchingly important. Since the expression of love is wrapped up in the meeting of needs, I can conclude that Bali loved me exceedingly well. And I loved her exceedingly well.

In the midst of my loss, I imagined God saying to me:

> *I brought Bali to you just as you were about to enter your physical and emotional struggles. She is home now. I know your heart is broken tonight. Don't stuff your feelings down. Let the goodness of her life wash over you. Thank you for loving her with such care. She trusted you with her entire heart.*
>
> *In her first year of life, she was turned against by her own*

mother and sister. It's why I gave her to you. She couldn't believe the goodness she fell into. I've heard Stacey say to you, "I don't believe in reincarnation, but if I did, I'd want to come back as John Lynch's dog." Oh, how I love that line!

Bali slept on the bed between you and Stacey most of her life—thank Stacey for me—I know how much she hates dog fur. You have proudly walked Bali through the same neighborhoods for so long. I know you are suddenly feeling like an old guy wandering the streets all alone. I'm not sure about you getting another dog... I know Stacey wants a cat, but you've had seven of those. They get hit by cars or stolen by old women from the nearby retirement community... (I realize that nobody has ever proven that, but you and I both know what happened! That lady was always petting Mija for far too long as she came by on her walks. One day, it was too much for her and she picked up that cat and carried her home. If it's any consolation, she was a big hit with the seniors out on the patio villas.)

You've had an incredible run, John. Most don't get such a relationship with an animal. And now, you get to love grandchildren. Give them snacks from the refrigerator—anything they want, and as much as they want. Just as you did for Bali.

2020

STACEY, CARLY, AMY, Cody, and the kids, Ridge and Navy, were all at San Clemente beach, on what was another typically astonishing Southern California afternoon in July. The undertow had been pretty strong that day. The lifeguards had already instructed us to move farther down the beach after telling us we had been swimming too close to the pier. But Ridge wanted to be in that ocean. So Cody and I decided to take him in. We were in pretty shallow surf and had already delivered multiple speeches about the danger of the currents. But still, five-year-old Ridge wanted to go further out than he ever had before. So out we go; Cody in front of him and me behind him. Now, I know what you're thinking... *What were you guys thinking?!* But for some reason, what we were doing seemed, if not safe, at least safe enough.

Suddenly, a wave surprised him and swept him off his feet towards shore. I'd seen this happen before. I knew it meant he would cry and that it would be the end of our fun. But instead, he came up laughing. He called out, to no one in particular, "Well, I guess Ridge is swimming now!"

Our eyes met as Cody and I both did a double-take. Ridge then noticed a particularly large wave forming off in the distance. With a giant smile, he yelled out, "Well, apparently we're all gonna die now!" What was going on? I knew this boy. In most areas of his life, Ridge was pretty cautious. Even when his parents would tell him that something was safe, it wasn't enough for Ridge. He would be the one who would decide if something was safe. Some kids require constant protection from breaking their arms and necks because they have no sense of personal danger. Not Ridge. But that day, in the wild and wooly surf, something was different. He appeared to have little caution.

Another wave swelled and sent his little body laughing towards the shore. "Yep, Ridge is swimming, again!" he laughed. I don't think I'd ever seen him more carelessly ecstatic. He was enjoying excitement like I enjoy excitement.

Here's my best take on what was happening; neither Cody or I were trying to convince Ridge that he didn't have to worry. Neither of us were writing the script for him. We were actually just about to call that whole adventure off just moments before and get us all back to the beach. But Ridge hadn't sized up that there was any danger in that situation. Ridge knew that Cody was in front of him to catch him if he tumbled. He knew that I was between him and the waves. And in that very moment, I think God was convincing Ridge that he was protected. Ridge had struggled in the early years of his life with allowing anyone to protect him. But in that moment, he was convinced that he had the freedom to pay attention to exhilarated fun, instead of fear. Cody and I looked at each other; it was decided, we were going to let this magical scene play out a bit longer.

When Ridge was done, he was done—but not because crying or fear made the decision for him. He had simply had enough wild surf for one day. That day's experience will neither cause Ridge to become irresponsible in the future, or stop him from feeling afraid in situations when he doesn't need to be. But for a moment, a boy's own understanding of safety allowed him to begin a new pattern of trust that may shape his entire life. One day, Ridge will become fully aware of what happened in San Clemente that day—he learned how to trust God with himself. And that pattern of trust will allow him to live out a powerful, and sometimes dangerous, adult destiny as he takes the costly risk to love and protect others. As he feels God surrounding him, he will laugh in the face of giant waves on the horizon. And as he does, though he knows better, he'll yell, "Well, apparently we're all gonna die now!" It will always be fun for him to say it.

. . . Awakening . . .

The only person that I will never be able to protect is me. I cannot see myself, or my situation, accurately. When I risk trusting myself to someone, the resulting response is playfulness that releases me into experiences that self-protection would never allow. This is true with God and with others we choose to trust. A great gift the mature can give one another is a safe place to try out new possibilities within the range of who God has made them to be.

2020

I HAVE NO idea how damaging the COVID-19 virus will have been by the time you read this book. Lately, nearly every day, I hear newscasters reminding their viewers that "those over sixty-five, with pre-existing conditions, are most susceptible to morbidity from this virus."

Hey, wait. That's me! When did that happen? Last time I checked, I was thirty-two and my only pre-existing condition was playful sarcasm. It suddenly occurred to me that I might not always be here. I am not immortal—some days, I am barely mortal. So, the next four stories you're about to read were written with the awareness that one day, maybe soon, I won't be here.

There are four parts to what I'm calling The COVID Quartet. First, I'll explain how I've felt my very best in this lifetime when I was trusting God to do what I would otherwise, not want to do. The second story reveals what cannot be taken away from us by the darkness and discusses what I can offer in the middle of dark times. The third is about God's intimate presence with us, no matter what, or where, we find ourselves. And then lastly, I would like to say goodbye to my wife.

2020

THERE IS A vast difference between ecstatic pleasure and what has, most surprisingly, sustained my heart. I can get ecstatic pleasure from a well-constructed bread pudding or a massage from an old merchant marine. But heart-brimming fulfillment?... The things that make up that list have surprised me, over and over.

Risking to reveal, and own, where I've been wrong or in need—even when it has cost me greatly—has given me some of the most significant meaning in my life. I would never have expected it to work that way.

The deepest part of the new me is explained, revealed, enjoyed, and proven best:

- when I own what I've done wrong.
- when I tell on myself.
- when I take a stand that could cost me significantly.
- when I risk telling another the sin I was intending to commit.
- when I am the first to approach the other to resolve an issue between us.
- when I let others protect me.
- when I let those I trust tell me truth about myself.
- when I allow myself to believe God loves me as I claim He does.
- when I trust the power of the resurrection to not let my worst

failures define me.

- when I allow God to shut down the voice that hisses at me that I'm innately too much, not enough, too messed up, too self-consumed, or too controlling.
- when I admit that I lied about something.
- when I let Jesus love me despite thinking I've messed up too many times.
- when I give up being right for doing right.
- when I stop reloading in an argument and instead, choose to listen.
- when I choose to trust God's assessment of me.
- when I choose to not hate one who has harmed someone dear to me.
- when I choose peace in the life God has given me and with those He has given me.
- when I find myself caring about others' needs more than my own.
- when I use my gifts for another's benefit.
- when I find myself counting influence as more important than importance.
- when I value destiny greater than personal success.
- when I value heaven more than earth without discounting a moment of life on this sacred planet.

2020

HAVE YOU EVER felt like you could make a significant contribution to something important as long as the world did its part and well... worked properly? I have. At times, that belief—that lack of feeling in control, and that feeling of having life just happen to me without my say—has caused me to become listless and frozen in place. This season wasn't supposed to happen, right?

These feelings have led me to take inventory of my situation, remind myself of the truth, and ask myself, what can't be taken away from me, no matter what? What is there for me to hold onto when all hell's breaking loose? Certain seasons of life can feel like a dam has broken and when a dam breaks, we know the next thing to come is for the village to flood. So what do I do when the dam breaks? And furthermore, if the flood comes and I discover I have survived it, what do I now have within me to uniquely give to others? These are big questions—big questions that we need answers to.

So, here is my best shot at answering these questions. I hope these truths will make a difference in your life, just as they have in mine.

When darkness comes and I face a season that takes me to my limits, I can hold onto these facts:

- God has created me uniquely, with wonderful purpose, and for this time, or He would have placed me in another season.
- He knows how to make my life count in any time period of

history.
- The goal of this life is to let Him love me, and for me to enjoy Him and others as I trust Him with me. This cannot be taken from me by anything external.
- Nothing will happen to me that the one who loves me more than myself, cannot bring good from.
- God will not let my life be wasted by any calamity.

Surviving difficult seasons uniquely equips me to offer hope and speak into the darkness that others might be facing because:

- I have been created uniquely to care for others in their unique circumstances, in a way no one else can.
- I have power in my new nature to offer life-giving hope to another.
- I can offer others a safe place to be real.
- I can offer a trusted place where sin loses its power.
- I know who I am in Him, I can give a place for others to grieve, with no timetable and no expectation of how they should grieve.
- I get to model playful authenticity, to give someone hope that they too can find joy in the season they're facing.
- I get to show people the real me, with all my particular wonder and quirks that He has formed in me, so they can feel confident to present the real them as well.
- I get to retell stories of God's faithfulness so that people will know that great good can come from a season that tries to convince you there is no good to be had.
- I get to show others my insecurity, fears, doubts, and imma-

turity, so they can become convinced there are no "together" people, and that God has all of us right on time.

These lists are truths that we can come back to every time we forget, if only for a moment, that Jesus has already, is currently, and will for the rest of our lives, swoop in and make things better.

2020

WHEN YOU AWAKEN in the middle of the night, and you can't turn off the noise—I am with you.

When your car breaks down on a cold, dark street, far from home—I am with you.

When news of sudden tragedy hits and in mind-numbing shock, you forget where you are—I am with you.

When others you thought were friends are found to have been undermining you—I am with you.

When you first discover a suspicious lump—I am with you.

When you are broken up with through a text—I am with you.

On My Worst Day

When you've been overheard speaking carelessly about someone you love—I am with you.

When you choose not to call the friend who could get you out of the wrong you're about to allow—I am with you.

When you're angry with Me for not fulfilling long-held dreams—I am with you.

When someone you love is making choices that have long-term consequences and you have no way in—I am with you.

When you feel listless, uninspired, and too tired to care—I am with you.

When your desires are changing and you don't know who to tell—I am with you.

When you are hurting yourself because you carry so much self-disgust—I am with you.

When you fear you may be losing your mind—I am with you.

When you embarrassingly fail at a presentation which was supposed to be the validation of your abilities and future—I am with you.

When you've been hiding something for so long you feel there is no way out—I am with you.

When you realize you can't stop medicating your pain—I am with you.

When you make promises to Me and break them all—I am with you.

When you've lost your faith and don't want it back—I am with you.

When you come to the end of your rope and there is nothing left to hold onto—I am with you.

When you cry out to Me, finally daring to risk for My can help—I am with you.

When you call someone in the dead of the night to whisper, "Help"—I am with you.

When you find yourself praying, not because you should, but because you want to—I am with you.

When you begin to distinguish My voice, from the voice of shame—I am with you.

When you catch yourself smiling—I am with you.

When you stop promising Me anything—I am with you.

When you find yourself no longer afraid of Me—I am with you.

When the feeling of hope returns, after you thought it was lost forever—I am with you.

When you discover you never have to perform for Me again—I am with you.

When you come to believe your sin has nothing to do with My affection or commitment to you—I am with you.

When you begin to trust My new life is fully alive within you—I am with you.

When you celebrate sobriety with a group of family and friends—I am with you.

When you see a long-forgotten dream come true—I am with you.

When you find the bravery to confess something you've been hiding for years to the one it affected the most—I am with you.

When you choose to risk living each day with no hard feelings towards anyone—I am with you.

When a family member asks if they can ride along just to be with you—I am with you.

When you are breathing your last breath and hoping everything you've believed is actually true—I am with you.

2020

STACEY,

I'm so happy that you're reading the words of this chapter for the first time after it's been published. For once, I get to be the one who patiently waits for the right moment to give a gift.

Every time I got on a plane in L.A. to visit you in Phoenix, you feared you'd watch the plane explode into a fireball as it taxied in. Now, here we are, thirty-five years later, and all my planes have landed safely.

From early on, you demanded that my love would be expressed. You demanded that I would not be rehearsed or disengaged. When we met, I was a young, immature Christian attending seminary. My heart was still guarded from years of brokenhearted wandering. I still remember driving around LAX with you, several months into our relationship. We had a few minutes left together before your flight back to Phoenix.

"John, what are you afraid of?" you asked me.

"What do you mean?"

You had been waiting for the perfect moment to say what came next.

"You're holding back. You're afraid you'll get hurt again, so you hold your heart at a distance. You allow yourself to commit right up to the level of my commitment, and no further. Look, John, I don't know about the girls who left you—but I am *not* them." You began crying quietly. The personal woundings I was still carrying with me were hurting you. In that moment, so much changed. You proved you could handle me, and that was the moment I risked everything and went all in.

Where would I be without you, Stacey? Though you knew I was a mess, you saw Jesus wildly in me. You saw a man who would protect your heart. You believed I could speak His Word and that lives would be changed. You believed you could teach me how to love children and to be all in.

No other person has shaped my life more. No one. And Bill Thrall has been my mentor!

Over time, you discovered just how fragile, insecure, frightened, weak, and unstable I could be. It never deterred you. You have learned how to offer your commitment even when I get lost in the world.

I think that my love and need of your goodness has changed how you respond when you get hurt. Just recently, we hurt each other's feelings. Inflamed, you could have chosen to say unkind words. Instead, you listened to me. You told me you were sorry. You meant it. You heard me. I got to hear you. It was like watching Philippians chapter two come alive. You were so strong, humble, and heroic to me.

You are more beautiful to me than ever. What is that about? You're not the twenty-six-year-old girl I first fell in love with. But the other morning, you walked out onto our patio as the sun was just coming up. You were in your white nightgown, carrying a cup of coffee; barely awake, smiling your contented grin. I had to say it, though it felt so cheesy and vulnerable. "Stacey, you look like an angel. I know you're not. But you are so beautiful to me."

We've had an astonishing life. I came from an atheist family, you a nominally Christian home. Yet, God has used us significantly, for many. We were immature and full of untested religious one-liners. I judged you for having too many shoes and wanting to dye your hair. I was such a Pharisee. Geesh! Again, I'm so sorry. Now I'm the one with a shoe issue, and asking you to make your hair blonder!

But you saw past all that. You knew who you were. And you could see past the religious poser in me, to a man who would trust God and learn to tell on himself.

I have applied myself to understand the workings of God's grace. I have given my life to know how love plays out. I have wanted to model and teach that God's grace is real and stronger than any other motivation to do right. That grace isn't a theology to defeat other theologies, but rather a way of living that I can trust in any season. I sometimes promise too much and speak in hyperbole. But I believe in the Jesus I offer to the frail and lonely and you have allowed me to walk out into that world where pain and confusion reside. You've never been resentful of my time away. You trusted my commitment to our family. You've never been fearful of anyone's praise of me. You know I don't have the chops for infidelity. I need my sleep. And I've never wanted anyone but you.

We've been to so many exotic places all over the world. We somehow rigged the system—middle-class folk on an extended working vacation. I often say that it's when we're on the road that we get to live like semi-wealthy people. It's at home where things break and the wine is less nice. But despite that fact, we're probably happiest when we're together in our middle-class home.

I have no fear that you won't continue to thrive without me. I've taught you to trust that good faith and good science will always overlap perfectly. I've taught you that *you*, Stacey Lynch, are eminently delightful. The instincts of your heart are wonderfully trustworthy and you are becoming wise. I can't wait to watch your influence continue to blossom.

Most importantly, you've placed your entire hope upon grace and your fused identity in Christ. Not because I teach it, not because Bill Thrall, Andrew Farley, or anyone else teaches it. God has taught *you*! How magnificent. You share it with such confidence to those God is giving you influence over.

You have always wanted others in our home. Before you, I was a recluse who wanted people to stay in their own homes. You've taught me to delight in helping host parties, celebrations, ministry events, and milestones. Thousands of people have experienced the grace of God on our patio, because of *you*.

If you end up having thirty more years after me, you will be cared for. So many love us. Grieve me for several weeks, but then you have my permission to get on with life. It will honor me if you do. You were created to be playful, to have FOMO, and to hike in beautiful places. Please don't marry the guy with the pencil-thin moustache who will spend our retirement savings on a vintage accordion and cases of thin, reedy Pinot Noir. Please...

Thank you. I cried writing those two words. I am convinced I would have compromised myself without the strength of your person, Stacey. Instead, we got to share that cup of coffee in Venice and raise a beautiful family in Phoenix. God used us, and continues to use us, to bless the lives of many. It has been so exceedingly better than anything either of us could have dreamed. I love you endlessly.

I can't wait to see what is up ahead. The magical, safe, kind, and wildly playful world I've told others about now awaits me. So, I finish this with the words I've written to you on hundreds of notes, letters, and cards throughout our years together... The rabbit's ears are still down.

John

2020

I'VE HAD MY share of good days on this planet. I've seen Koufax pitch. Sandy *freaking* Koufax! I performed the "Two Roads" talk with MercyMe, in a majestic Baltimore theater, while on tour with them. I've eaten buttermilk pie—warm buttermilk pie. A butterfly once landed on my finger after I asked it to. I've watched humans land on the moon. I've caught countless white bass with a leather-armed guide named Hank. At a wedding reception, Stacey Marie Pilger flirted with me and it changed my entire life. I've seen Bruce Cockburn perform, on five separate evenings. I've sat on the bow of a catamaran with Charlie Millard, our legs dangling overboard, watching flying fish for an entire hour. I performed a wedding on a bluff next to Moraine Lake, at the foot of the Canadian Rockies. I watched my son win state in the 800-meter run. Twice. And sitting at a table with a crisp linen tablecloth, on the edge of the Grand Canal in Venice, Stacey and I sipped the finest cup of coffee either of us had ever tasted.

I've also had great days. Deeply meaningful days. Days when my life on this planet counted. I once saved one of my best friends from drowning in a river. I beat up a bully. I was used by God to keep someone from committing suicide. I've preached in the church I used to pastor, as a guest preacher, for the present pastor, my son.

All of us could list some good and great days. But what would a best day look like? I think a best day would be the experience of Him taking one of our worst days and bringing it to redemption. Maybe, a best day is one that we'd lost hope would ever come to pass.

I'd like to share with you one last story. The story of my best day—a worst day redeemed.

Stacey and I were invited to a friend's birthday party. I didn't want to go. We had something earlier in the evening, so we wouldn't be able to get there until after nine. At nine, there are usually blankets over me and the lights are turned off.

The party was somewhere in the far East Valley. So, even if we drove by and shouted, "Happy birthday, Doug," blankets would not be on me until after ten-fifteen. Doug Glynn is a pastor and I've preached at his church several times, so when we arrived, I was immediately greeted by many on the patio. But there was this one guy near the edge of the yard, staring at me like I either owed him money, or he owed me his life. He looked like he could ruin my plan of getting out of here quickly. He stood to approach me. "Hey, you don't know me, and I don't want to dominate your time, but would you mind coming out front with me? I really need to talk to you."

Nobody seemed to be noticing. I could see Stacey chatting it up with several in the kitchen. "Sure, I'd be happy to talk with you." What I really wanted to say was, "Are you aware I live forty miles from here and generally have been in bed for fifteen minutes already?" The front yard was poorly lit. No one was going to leave any time soon. He could've knifed me and it might be hours before anyone noticed. He got up close to my face. He looked manic. He was sweating and nervously looking around to see if anyone was watching. I started praying triple-speed. "God, help! Protect me. You see this guy, right?"

"Look," he said, far too quickly, "I know this seems strange. Give me two or three minutes. I've waited for this moment for two years. My name is Mark. My wife, Tracy, is here tonight. We're a miracle story. We shouldn't be here. Alive. We've had such horribly hard lives. I've tried to take my life. In junior high, I met the man who would later groom me and molest me. I became addicted to drugs and alcohol. My wife was sexually molested and physically abused by her stepdad almost daily from age nine to fourteen. We were married at sixteen and seventeen, and have been together for forty years. Most of those years, we were in shattered, relational brokenness. We have been homeless with our three children. We are both recovered meth addicts." I was regretting my judgment of this man. He was heroic.

"So, I wandered into Doug's church and found these people. They have drawn our hearts to God. Two years ago though, I was still so new at this... you know how you come to know God, but the ugliness doesn't just leave right away? Sexual abuse, it messes up the picture you have of who you really are. Like you're never going to be enough. Like you aren't worth it to have someone respect you enough not to ruin you. You always feel like God has to endure you.

"Some time ago, I received a phone call from Doug inviting me to watch a movie with a group of guys. The thoughts of suicide stirred in my head, as they still sometimes do. I didn't want to go. But I went."

Mark yelled, as if I was across the street, "Dude, you're in it! You're in the movie! *The Heart of Man.*" He now had his hands firmly on my shoulders, kindly shaking me. I was mesmerized. God was not only doing this for Mark. He was doing this for me. I suddenly couldn't wait to hear where this story would go.

"Anyway, it gets to the section in the movie where you tell your story about getting violated in fifth grade. I froze in my chair. Someone was telling my story. Someone knew! I was watching a man admit his life was horribly changed one day in a boxcar. John, I don't have words to describe what I felt, watching you share your brokenness. But then you started talking about experiencing healing from

Jesus—how you no longer saw yourself as an unneeded failure—I had never seen that before. How could it be? How could you possibly see yourself so free? Not me. Never, not ever fully for me. But, sitting there in the dark, God was convincing me you were telling the truth. At that very moment, something changed. I knew I would never be the same. I believed God could do the same for me. At that moment, I wanted to stand up in that room and yell, 'Do you hear this? Do you hear this guy?! I'm going to be okay. This guy is me! Swear to God, I'm going to make it.'

"John, God used you to convince me that I was redeemable. I'm not ever going to have to take my life. He's freed me from the lie that I'm not enough to be loved." My hands were now on his shoulders. We both started to cry. "I knew I had to meet you. Then you showed up here tonight. I'm sorry I scared you."

I can't remember much of what I said to him. I do, however, know that I was undone by what God was doing through him at that moment. In the front yard of a place I did not want to be, this guy was revealing the repainting of my story. God had been weaving this story a long time. I had no idea there was a Mark Sullivan out there in the world, who was going through hell. I had no idea that he would eventually find an authentic community, and would later see my story in a movie. I had no idea that God would use my story to free his very person. I had no idea that by him telling me that my life had counted in his, I would suddenly become freer than I'd ever been. We hugged each other fiercely. Two men long ago robbed of innocence by sick people. Both men disgusted and ashamed with themselves for so long. And now, here we were. Free men. Strong and unchained, in Christ. Alive men. Wounded healers, helping free others robbed by sick people.

The entire way home I kept hearing the words play over in my mind, "John, God used you to convince me that I was redeemable. I'm not ever going to have to take my life." God did it. He redeemed my very worst day with the redemption of another. Redemption: to liberate by payment, to release from debt or blame, to offset, to override the bad effect.

Doug gives me Mark's contact information. I want him to help me get the story right. Mark and I text back and forth like we are still in the front yard of that party. Mark ended our text conversation with these words: "Praying your words find many more Mark Sullivans. My life today is so amazing. I love myself today. I am worthy of love. There are so many hurting people. I want to try to reach as many as I can as well… I love helping others."

This pattern is true for each of us. Every single day, every failed moment, every chronic, drawn-out, unresolved, anxious time, during every nap on the couch—He is magnificently, and surgically, redeeming your worst days into your best ones. God is healing other Mark Sullivans so they can be placed in front of you and used in the redemption story of your worst day. It will catch you off guard, and happen on a day when you aren't looking for it.

I imagine Jesus saying this to me;

John, one of the things I adore about you most is your bravery. You have trusted Me with the results of the boxcar story. You lived all the way to this night never knowing if you'd see any payoff from all the pain and loss that horrific violation cost you. You have trusted Me to believe you are clean and righteous, and that you are loved as much as anyone I have ever loved. Yet, you'd never experienced anyone articulate what you went through could be used in their healing. You've waited fifty-five years to hear Mark's words. You tend to stuff things down, so we have not talked much about that day in fifth grade. I experienced that day completely with you. Since that day, I have experienced every hiding, every posturing, every lonely doubt that you would ever be enough for another, with you. The lingering thought that there is something uniquely and irreparably wrong with you—you may have thought you were alone— but you never were. Redemption is not a tenet of cold theology. It is a relational experience, between a human and God. Or humans and God. You experienced it when you dared to believe this event did not define who you are; that you have been liberated from its power and bad effect. Redemption is released when someone believes the power of the cross and resurrection is stronger than what happened to them. John Lynch, My son, tonight we celebrate this together. The fact that it's after eleven and you are still not in bed; that's on you. I love you.

And so the story continues. For all of us. Not a minute left to chance, not a moment uncared for. Our role is to stay in the moment and not miss any of it. The one who loves you more than you are capable of loving yourself has gone up ahead. He turns back to face you and offers you a smile to give you the courage to fully enter into the next moment—the next turn in the road. Even if, like me, it takes fifty-five years for redemption to enter in and change your narrative, there will be great gifts of His goodness along the way. We get to just sit back and drink it all in—even the worst days—as we trust Him to redeem them into our best ones.

Acknowledgments

I NEVER THOUGHT I'd get the chance to write nearly forty new stories and extend the timeline for *On My Worst Day*. But I have discovered there are many like me, who have been defined by their worst days, and are now hungering to experience God's redemption of them.

Presenting this book to you makes me feel like one of the most fortunate people on the planet. But I'd never be able to risk these vulnerable stories without a close circle of friends and family God uses to hold me together.

Stacey—During our entire marriage, you have sacrificially allowed me to pursue the uneven journey of writing and speaking. One day an author can knock out fifteen pages, the next day half a paragraph. While I am hunkered down in my office, you gladly and joyfully carry so much of our world. While other husbands can build and repair things, you are married to a man overmatched by a variable speed belt sander. Oh, how I love you.

Caleb, Amy, and Carly—You have each proven, in your own uniquely meaningful lives, that this grace and love of Jesus we have tried out in our family actually works. I hope the words I have written about you three are honoring to each of you. Kali, thanks for loving

Caleb so well and for allowing us to stand with you in loving Maci and Payton. Cody, thank you for protecting Amy so well and letting us have a significant role as you parent Ridge and Navy.

My board of John Lynch Speaks—You have believed in me and this message of grace and identity in Jesus. You have each boldly lived out this way of life. You have protected me and actively walked this journey with me. I do not do any of this without you.

When some authors write a book, they need a proofreader. When I write a book, I need a concept editor, a line editor, a content editor, a copy editor, a text editor, a form editor, and a reality editor. (I made that last one up.) This book is produced and marketed entirely by Lazarus Media Productions. Josh Gordon, you only wanted to help me figure out how to get these truths out, whether I joined up with you or not. You convinced me your team understood these truths of grace and were trying them out in their families. Sarah Brown and the rest of you have done such a great job creating my website, brand, and all manner of social media. But your greatest gift to me has been Amber O'Brien and Amy Cowhard. They both have taken on this book as a labor of love. You two are both incredibly professional and skilled at your craft, but you have owned this project like it was your own. Amy, you looked up obscure baseball player references just to get the spelling right, and you found the make and model of a bicycle just to give the piece authenticity. You're incredible. And Amber... I don't know what to say. You have believed in this book, sometimes maybe even more than I have. (I just teared up writing that last sentence.) Thank you.

Mark Sullivan—Thank you for allowing me to tell your story.

Dennis, Cindy, Michael, and Kristen—Thank you so, so much for allowing me to tell David's story.

Bob Ryan and Caleb—Thank you for helping me bring these

stories to the stage in "Live at Borsodi's."

Open Door Fellowship—Thank you for continuing to be a community fighting to relevantly model and teach "Christ in us" to our culture and the faith community all over the world.

And thank you to everyone who has ever put a like or a heart on anything I have ever posted on Facebook or Instagram. Like moths drawn to light, we are finding each other.

To all my grace author friends—Well done. You each inspire me. I am your fan.

And to Jesus—My God, my best friend, hero, and the one I cannot live without. Thank You for allowing me to imagine what You might be saying, throughout this book, and throughout my life.

REFERENCES

[1] Martin, S. 2007. Born Standing Up: A Comic's Life. Simon & Schuster. pp. 188.

[2] O'Malley, Joseph, translator. Critique of Hegel's 'Philosophy of the Right' by Karl Marx. 1970. Cambridge University Press. pp. 131.

[3] Nouwen, H. 1988. Letters to Marc About Jesus. Harper Collins. pp. 4.

ABOUT THE AUTHOR

Since 1985, serving at Open Door Fellowship, Trueface, and now John Lynch Speaks, John has been writing, speaking, and acting out all manner of media on trusting our new, shame-free identity in Jesus and receiving His endless grace and love.

He is perhaps best known for his dramatic presentations of the "Two Roads" message and co-authoring *The Cure*. He has co-authored five other books, including *Bo's Café*, *The Cure and Parents*, *Trust For Today*, *TrueFaced*, and *Beyond Your Best*. *On My Worst Day* is his first solo effort.

John co-founded and for fifteen years helped write, direct and act in Sharkey Productions, a Gospel-anchored theater group, eventually performing in the prestigious Herberger Theater. With the release of the updated *On My Worst Day*, John is performing "Live at Borsodi's", a one-person show based on stories from this book.

He currently teaches the practical implications of this new life in

Jesus, through a growing library of short videos and social media insights with John Lynch Speaks.

John and Stacey absolutely delight in their real, meaningful, and very playful marriage. They love each other and delight in their friends, in Phoenix and beyond. Stacey travels with John more and more on his speaking events. She loves to meet others and enter into their lives but refuses to teach in almost any setting. John has tried. Oh, so many times.

John and Stacey both cherish their three children, Caleb, Amy, and Carly. Caleb is married to a deeply empathetic Kali, and Amy is married to a wonderfully faithful Cody. The Lynchs have four grandchildren, Maci, Payton, Ridge, and Navy. All of this family is marvelously interwoven throughout this book and throughout John and Stacey's lives.

John carries dreams of writing his next book, *On My Best Day*. He and Stacey have always longed to provide a safe place, personally in their home and virtually throughout the world, for friends to be real and full of the freedom that comes from being endlessly loved. This will forever be their hearts' desire.

Made in the USA
Middletown, DE
17 February 2023

25096388R00199